IN THE

CONVERSATIONS WITH EIGHT CANADIAN POETS

ESSAY SERIES 58

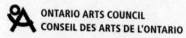

Guernica Editions Inc. acknowledges the support
of the Canada Council for the Arts and the Ontario Arts Council.
The Ontario Arts Council is an agency of the Government of Ontario.

LAURENCE HUTCHMAN

IN THE WRITERS' WORDS

**CONVERSATIONS WITH EIGHT
CANADIAN POETS**

GUERNICA
Toronto·Buffalo·Lancaster (U.K.)
2011

Copyright © 2011, Laurence Hutchman, The Authors and Guernica Editions Inc.
All rights reserved.
The use of any part of this publication, reproduced, transmitted in any form or by any means, electronic, mechanical, photocopying, recording or otherwise stored in a retrieval system, without the prior consent of the publisher is an infringement of the copyright law.

Antonio D'Alfonso, editor
Guernica Editions Inc.
P.O. Box 117, Station P, Toronto (ON), Canada M5S 2S6
2250 Military Road, Tonawanda, N.Y. 14150-6000 U.S.A.

Distributors:
University of Toronto Press Distribution,
5201 Dufferin Street, Toronto (ON), Canada M3H 5T8
Gazelle Book Services, White Cross Mills, High Town, Lancaster LA1 4XS U.K.

First edition.
Printed in Canada.

Legal Deposit – First Quarter
Library of Congress Catalog Card Number: 2010936046
Library and Archives Canada Cataloguing in Publication
In the writers' words : conversations with eight Canadian
poets / Laurence Hutchman, editor.
(Essay series ; 58)
ISBN 978-1-55071-309-1.
Poets, Canadian (English) – 20th century – Interviews.
2. Canadian poetry (English) – 20th century – History and criticism.
I. Hutchman, Laurence II. Series: Essay series (Toronto, Ont.) ; 58
PS8155.I57 2011   C811'.5409   C2010-905958-1

CONTENTS

In the Writers' Words: An Introduction   7

Ralph Gustafson   11

George Johnston   30

P.K. Page   48

Fred Cogswell   71

Louis Dudek   88

Al Purdy   116

Anne Szumigalski   134

James Reaney   159

Acknowledgements   185

Biographical Notes   186

For Mary

IN THE WRITERS' WORDS: AN INTRODUCTION

This book of interviews is a collection of some of the most influential poets of the modern and postmodern period in Canadian literature. These poets made important contributions and laid essential groundwork for younger poets who followed them. I conducted all but one of these interviews in the 1990s. These interviews have been published in journals, but those journals are not readily available.

Ralph Gustafson, with his ironic poems, witnesses the world, and gives us novel ideas about beauty. Fred Cogswell's Quebecois and Acadian translations and George Johnston's translations of Norwegian and Faroese make other literatures available to us. Both of them have written witty, satirical poems that have contributed to modern Canadian literature. P.K. Page explores the complexities of the psychological and aesthetic transformation of the spirit through formal poetry. Al Purdy, through his colloquial multi-toned voice and his original metaphors, shows how to incorporate our geography and history into poetry. Louis Dudek speaks about the publishing tradition in Canada and evokes new ways of looking at the world in his long poems. Anne Szumigalski evokes a visionary poetics that considerably enriches the poetry of the prairies. James Reaney demonstrates the essential qualities of the local landscape in *The Red Heart*.

When I interviewed these poets I read their poetry, other works they had written and articles and reviews that were written about them. I interviewed the poets in their homes, an integral part of them. There were surprises. The day the interview took place with Anne Szumigalski, the outer wall of her dining room was being repaired, so part of the interview was conducted with our coats on, until it got too cold and too noisy and we had to retire to her study.

In general I taped the conversations, except in the case of George Johnston, who thought the interview would be more natural if I wrote it longhand. I posed specific questions, but also left room for the conversation to follow its own course. I asked questions about the development of the poets' writing career, the writers who influenced them, the importance of place, literary theory, translation and the genesis of a poem.

Many of these interviews took place toward the end of these poets' lives. Ralph Gustafson talked about his early life in Canada with Charles G.D. Roberts and F.O. Call. And he spoke about his time at Oxford. I was fascinated with the period when

Gustafson lived in New York, his parties with A.J.M. Smith and Leon Edel, his meeting with William Carlos Williams in the Gotham Book Mart, and his return to Canada. Louis Dudek also spoke of his time in New York, and his sense of mission when he returned to Montreal to help create the city's rich poetry scene of the 1960s. I was interested in tracing the development from the early poems, through the longer poems of *Europe*, *En Mexique*, and *Atlantis*, into the later experiments with a series of poems such as *Continuations*.

Each of these writers expressed a strong sense of their own lives within the larger context of history. What the writers say about their craft, in these interviews, I hope, gives a portrait of their lives. These poets created the path that Canadian literature took in subsequent years.

RALPH GUSTAFSON

It's grey and icy as I drive to the Eastern Townships on this, the second last day of December. North Hatley, known as a centre for English Quebec poets, is located at the end of Lake Massawippi. It is a steep drive up the short street where Ralph Gustafson lives. Locally, it is known as the "Rue des Écrivains," since his neighbours are D.G. Jones and Ronald Sutherland, writers and teachers at the University of Sherbrooke nearby. Ralph Gustafson lives at the end of the road and his home, a cosy two-storey wooden house with a cedar hedge around it and a flower garden at the back, appears to be almost one with the tree-covered hill.

Ralph greets me at the door with its view of the distant lake and asks if I have had a hard drive. Inside, the living room is warm and Ralph comments, "You need a fire on the hearth on a day like this afternoon of winter," as he puts another birch log on the fire. He introduces me to Betty, his wife, as full of welcome and consideration as he is. They met when he was working in broadcasting in New York City.

At the opposite end of the room from the fireplace, against the staircase to the upstairs bedrooms, is a medium sized Steinway grand piano. Along the far side of the living room, bookshelves extend to the ceiling, full of poetry and novels; three middle shelves hold Ralph's books of poetry and the books in which his work has appeared. From a beam over the entrance to an alcove with windows, desk and flowers devoted to his wife, are Christmas decorations.

On the mantel framing the fireplace stands a small clay horseman from the Chinese Tang dynasty; a replica in relief of the Egyptian pharaoh Akhenaten, "the first individual in history"; a porcelain satirical modeling of Hamlet, seated, consulting the deceased jester Yorick's skull; Orrefors vases from Sweden; and elongated nude Etruscan figures, two of them, "ombra della sera," from Italy. To the side of the mantel hangs a watercolour of the Grand Canal in Venice, and a leaf from a notebook of Ruskin, which Ralph bought in the Lake District when he was at Oxford. All of this is a wondrous mixture of lands and cultures and emotions which Ralph shows me, observing, "No matter the diversity, all things of beauty harmonize."

On the coffee table are *The Mind of God, The Celestial Harmonies, Canadians in Venice*, and *Phineas*

Finn, cream, a silver sugar dredger for the hot coffee to come and dark chocolate Bahlsen Waffeltten.

Ralph leads me into the music room. Shelves again to the ceiling holding one of the best collections of piano recordings anywhere: 78 rpms, direct cuts from Saint-Saëns to Rachmaninoff, a collection which Ralph has donated and is about to go to the National Library in Ottawa. On the wall is a framed coloured photograph of Michelangelo's "God Creating Adam," from the Sistine Chapel ceiling in the Vatican, and a Chinese contemplative pastel of winter. On a bookshelf above the recessed TV are videos of Charlie Chaplin.

In the hallway is a picture of Lime Ridge, the village in the St. Francis River Valley, Wolfe County, where Ralph Gustafson was born.

*

You completed a Master of Arts degree at Bishop's University in Lennoxville, Quebec, and wrote your thesis on Keats and Shelley. What effect did these poets have on you?

In the short run, a deep effect. In the mature run, a diminishing influence. I started off very romantically. At that ancient time sixty years ago the university's official survey of poetry stopped at Swinburne. I was fortunate in coming under the personal interest of a

Canadian poet on the Faculty, F.O. Call, so that I was awakened by such figures as Vachel Lindsay and his "Boomlay, Boomlay, Boom" on the drums in his poem "The Congo," and Carl Sandburg, piling his bodies high at Austerlitz and Gettysburg. The drums and carnage grabbed me, but the "Ode on a Grecian Urn" and Browning's "Fra Lippo Lippi" were paramount. I was thrown too emphatically on the loves that an isolated youth has for romantic emulation. I was held captive in the nineteenth century, against my instinct to break loose. At the heart of the emulation was language as a musical expression. I had yet to know how to put into expression the emotional context of what was immediately around me personal and social. The superb use of sensual language that early poetic figures had, which eventually found entry and revitalization in Gerard Manley Hopkins, made entry about the time of my graduation, through the presentations of the then poet laureate Robert Bridges to whom my tutor, Professor W.O. Raymond, the Browning expert, sent my initial poems. Bridges died shortly after reading them!

There was a connection between the two events.

Bridges was envious.

So your time at Bishop's didn't leave you unprepared for the twentieth century.

Indeed not. I had a grounding in literature and history more wonderful than a computer, a personal relationship that technology can't approach. Natural tradition must not be lost. Conventions, okay, scrap them if they don't fit. But that tendency today to deconstruct what is valid is stupid. Tradition makes possible a vital evolution. That, I sensed, was what Oxford had.

A contact with the long-living tradition of English literature.

It cost me a year more for my degree. I was a test case for Oxford raising its regard for universities abroad, like Bishop's, from junior to senior status. Instead of two, I had to take three years to get another BA. The senior status subsequently came through, but it really wouldn't have made much difference in an awareness of contemporary poetry. The Oxford curriculum stopped short at the beginning of the century, too. What happened was that I could then hear world authorities on past literature: Professor Saintsbury on Matthew Arnold, for instance. What was of permanent poetic value to me was Oxford's demand that I learn the history of the English language, the inherent elements of the tongue I speak: such poems as the Middle English *Sir Gawain and the Green Knight* edited by Tolkien; above all, that Old English glory, *Beowulf*. I learned that the excitement of the Jesuit poet Manley Hopkins' "sprung rhythm," among the 1930s poets, was nothing but the Anglo Saxon poetic craft of *Beowulf*. The Canadian poet A.J.M. Smith later on was to say I wrote poetry like "a married Hopkins." Mix all that up with Browning and Pound, and you have the tradition I write by, successfully or not.

Today people often ignore that crucial tradition.

Broken prose and tin ears. Where I walked in Oxford was where Addison walked and Shelley tried to disseminate his atheism by floating poetic pamphlets by balloon out of his window at University College. I adhere to both attitudes: tranquility and madness. It was that paradox that I absorbed at Oxford. It was the beginning of my being contemporary with myself.

And you were influenced by the politically engaged poets.

Had to be. That was the time I was in, the context into which I was pitched, Europe in the 1930s. Graduating, I was writing my first book, *Flight into Darkness*, during my years in London. I had known of Roy Campbell, the South African poet, while I was at Oxford. He was shooting bullets at Stephen Spender in the Spanish Civil War. My adherence was "a plague on all your houses." I was anti-violence. One of the best poems I have written, "Basque Lover," was written then. The solution: love. The craft I used was that of the World War I poet, Wilfred Owen, the sorrowed half-rhyme. I wrote a whole section of *Flight into Darkness* called "Sequence to War," poetry about the war sirens being tried out in St. James Park among Wordsworth's daffodils. It looked like a flight into darkness. I was finished with the nineteenth century.

Was that a painful discovery?

Yes and no, social homicide and vital poetry.

Were there any other artists who influenced you to change perspective?

In music, Stravinsky. In painting, Kandinsky. In prose, D.H. Lawrence. People largely unknown in Canada. I remember smuggling, in a brown paper wrapper, a copy of Lawrence's *Lady Chatterley's Lover* that I bought in Oslo, Norway. Pound was running around Paris and Italy, like a clown. I tried to catch up with him in Rapallo and in Venice, without success. Those London years were all a sea change.

The twentieth century was changed.

Imagination. Habit and complacence were dislodged. I was reading Dickens' novel *Dombey and Son*. The first dozen chapters are almost a parody in Dickens' own manner. Then on page two hundred and fourteen, instead of saying Mr. Morfin of the Dombey firm was getting grey, Dickens says his dark hair was just touched here and there with specks of grey, "as though the tread of Time had splashed it." Imagination, in like manner, alerted the beginning of the twentieth century.

A touchstone of your style is the wide number of writers, artists and musicians that you tap in your work and use as resources.

I can't move about the world without being moved to expression by the creative glories of mankind, particularly the composers of music, more than the poets of words, perhaps. Music, the most exalting of the arts. I have pursued it from Haydn's Vienna to Chopin's Paris, from Wagner's Bayreuth to Bali's gamelan in geography. Music and the stars. I've written my epitaph:

> Astrophysicist
> And Ferenc Liszt
> He wanted to be.
> He settled the matter
> With poetry.

Good enough. To pursue your question: Yes, my poetry is rich with allusions to the great things mankind has achieved. I have been criticized for having too many so-called "references" to so-called "artifacts" in my verse. Allusions, yes, but not illusions. With the sordidness now about us, why not?

You have a strong sense of being politically engaged in your work. Did this start in the thirties?

The utter fatuity of Chamberlain coming back and waving that piece of paper, "peace in our time," that he had just signed with Hitler in Munich, was motivation enough for a lifetime. A deep strain of irony got in my verse: the utter disgust expressed later, in such poems as "The Newspaper" in *Corners in the Glass*, and in the poem "State of Affairs" in

Directives of Autumn. The titles of my books are enough indication. I have two prose pieces in my book of essays *Plummets and Other Partialities,* largely unread, that are politically concerned; one essay I called "Witness Poetry." The business of the world about him is the poet's business and has been since Milton wrote about the sorrows of the Piedmontese in the seventeenth century. In the thirties, Garcia Lorca commended his artist friend for "always putting your finger on the wound." Poetry sets the world to rights. Why don't people read it? Sarajevo, eliminated. The other partiality in my book of prose pieces is "Poetry as a Moral Procedure." Perhaps people don't read anymore. They only stare at Picasso's "Guernica." We are maimed by TV.

Did your being a member of the British Information Service in New York during World War II heighten this?

The question was would the world survive? Would the United States enter the World War? England had to know. The New York office had to have a legally neutral resident. The poet Leo Cox, in Montreal, recommended me. I had been inducted into the U.S. army. Myopia and the BIS request for a deferment on my behalf resulted in my being stationed in the offices in the RCA building in Rockefeller Center for the duration. I learned cablese, surveyed the U.S. radio networks and the newspaper chains and sent a nightly report of the fluctuating opinion in the States on the war, in time for the British Cabinet meeting in London the next morning. I assessed everything from columnist Kaltenborn, Father Coughlin, and the *Chicago Tribune* in the Midwest to Edward R. Murrow, wrote it up and had it cabled to England. I learned a very great deal.

And you kept on writing poetry and meeting American editors and poets.

That whole literary amalgamation, British and American, occurred. I wrote that pamphlet *Poetry and Canada* for the Canadian Legion Educational Services. Through Col. Bovey, registrar at McGill at that time, I edited the first version of the *Penguin Anthology of Canadian Verse* for Allen Lane in England – 60,000 copies of Canadian poetry all over the world! I wrote about Canadian poetry for "Life and Letters" in England, for the *Saturday Review of Literature* in the States. The point I am making is not to blow trumpets, but to say that, as a poet, I didn't feel alien anywhere. Milton Wilson, the Canadian critic, long ago pointed out that the advantage of being a Canadian is to have perspective toward Europe and toward the New World. While maintaining that, I emphasized that we are also ourselves. I wanted to walk in Venice without losing myself, which I can; I wanted to live in North Hatley within thirty miles of the Vermont border, which I do. I spoke at a symposium arranged by A.J.M. Smith at Michigan State University and asked, "Does the United States need to be provincial?"

You had long personal relationships with A.J.M. Smith and other poets.

We were both compiling anthologies of Canadian poetry; my Penguin beat his Chicago by a year. Arthur Smith was on a sabbatical in New York. I remember one supper with him and Jeannie when they were staying on West End Avenue. A couple of ladies of the night, above his dining room, were entertaining their boyfriends so joyously that the ceiling of plaster fell in on his son Peter's cradle. Leon Edel, biographer of Henry James, was in New York, as was the Montreal poet, Leo Kennedy. We went to Minsky's Burlesque on Broadway for objectivity. At Louis Untermeyer's invitation, at Leon Edel's, at Arthur Stringer's (a once-popular Canadian who wrote copiously), at Harold Vinal's, I spoke on the excellence of Canadian poetry at the New York Public Library, at Penn, at the Poetry Society of America, and where else?

Those were heady days. I was an habitué at the gathering place of all good writers, the Gotham Book Mart on 47th Street. One afternoon William Carlos Williams walked in seeking the advice of that stalwart of all good writing, the owner Frances Steloff, where he could get his poems published. I was astounded. If he couldn't, what hope for me? I wrote a short story, "The Human Fly," about a man, as a stunt, climbing the face of a building in Sherbrooke, Quebec, and sent it off without solicitation to *The Atlantic Monthly*. The editor, Edward Weeks, phoned me that the story was so good it made him dizzy and sent me a cheque for $300, higher pay than W.C. Williams got! Somerset Maugham read my poems. He said, alas, if he could only write poems! Name-dropping? Indeed not. All was real. Seven stories were chosen by Martha Foley, two winners published, five listed as distinguished in her *Best Short Stories of the Year*. Another in Whit Burnett's *Story Magazine*. And so on. Canada didn't pay any attention. I always thought the quality of poems written would establish the poems but of course I was, if dedicated, naive. Who you don't know won't do it.

We need a tough, respected critic . . .

. . . like Edmund Wilson of those days. I knew him too, but never mind. I was learning a craft and getting experience. The necessary things are love and a sense of comedy. I have got to the apex of my craft following that precept.

What is that?

The world has searched for years and has failed to find a rhyme for the word "orange." Leonard Cohen proposes "door-hinge." That won't do. But I have done away with any more quantum leaps, "Your pottage is oranger / Than that in my porringer."

During the 1940s the "little magazine" became more important in Canada.

Even though I was in New York and not in Toronto, I was still very concerned and implicated in that advance: as correspondent for *Northern Review* and advocate for that resplendent *Here and Now*. I knew all the *Preview* crowd, Patrick Anderson; A.M. Klein; Frank Scott, a close friend of mine; Canon Scott, Frank's father, who used to capture me in a corner of the gymnasium at Bishop's University and spout his poems at me. The whole group of *Preview* was fighting with John Sutherland and his "other Canadians" in *First Statement*. I sort of had a foot in both camps. Quality over sectionalism again, I suppose. That encouraging and exciting period was a change from the near isolation of creative writers from their audience. Then came the amalgamation of *Northern Review* and *Tamarack Review* and above all, the Canada Council.

In an interview in 1979 you said, "Personality in poetry is fine but there must be a projection beyond the personal element a comprehension of the world."

"An awareness of the world" would have been a better way of putting it than a "comprehension." Who comprehends the violence and vulgarity of our present context? The point I was making, of course, was that one's grandmother dies and so a poem about it must be written; you find accumulated dust behind the radiator and that's symbolic of your life.

Confessional poetry.

All of those clichés of birth, marriage and death,

the great denominators of poetry that are provisional, but not solipsistic. The poet should write out of his own experience, not sit in it. He should show how much more he loves language than his grandmother.

You were critical of a number of "new wave" younger Canadian poets in one of your prefaces.

A good friend of mine and a first-rate critic, Bruce Whiteman, writes prose poems. I said why not call the pieces poetic prose. He won my tender heart by saying, couldn't I love a little centaur? I love centaurs, and probably their poems, if they're like mine. You have to have feet in a poem, not necessarily four, but metre. Lines massed or scattered down a page won't do. A poem has to be freedom confronting challenge. To change the metaphor, there is no tennis with the net down. The emotion of rhythm playing across the pulse of metre, that's the essential of a poem. That, plus the meaning stated in the music of the language used. All must cohere. There is no drama without tension. Where do you break a line? Let the reader shout, "I have got it!" Don't make the reader write the poem . . . with which words, I quit defining the aesthetics and myself. "Technique is a test of a poet's sincerity," says Uncle Ez.

Poetry is a crafty business.

You can well use that pun . . . endless, even though you've "arrived" at your style.

Your work has long had a maturity of technical confidence. How does a poem come to you?

Ambition. I write poetry to complete myself, that double delight. Having become possessed by a need to clarify and to order an emotion derived out of personal experience, the initiation is intuitive: a phrase given, a ready style, a maturity of practice. The phrase is often the whole first line of what is to be a poem, "the given line," a line of music accurate for the emotion. The springboard can be a word I want to use and haven't so far, though that sort of singularity means a challenge that is formidable: a poem justifying such a beginning. Environment plays a necessary and a silly part in this whole business of genesis. The furniture of a room, its silence, comfort, view, isolation, familiarity, its strangeness. Whatever ... the routine or the dislocation. And, of course, whether or not you have indigestion, a cold, cancer or have forgotten to brush your teeth or something as asinine as not having paid a bill. Any excuse for not having to face the apocalypse of writing a poem.

You use the word "love" frequently in your poems.

The secret of happiness. I'm careful though, about overusing the word "love." The four letters have come to mean almost anything. It's become hypocrisy. "Beauty" is another such word. My solution is often to substitute the word "accuracy."

... which means to care.

Beauty is accuracy, the motivation of a poem. Its success is often called "inspiration." The force of that is a deliberate love of life.

That deliberate love of life comes through in all of your social poems, what you call "witness poetry."

You can't eliminate. I can't conceive of existence of any importance without love in it. It indicates the horrors of history. I write about a train blown up in the Brenner tunnel of Italy, of a man, a child, his leg blown off by a land mine. They are love poems. We stop at the fact and not the meaning.

You often suggest, in your poetry, that what is insurmountable in life does have an answer.

Never acquiesce. I don't like presenting the word "courage" as the thing to use or acquire. The word reverberates with patronage, namely, I have it and you must have it. Bravado repulses me. I disguise courage with comedy. The little fellow gets kicked in the seat of his pants, always, but he still loves the gal. Indomitability. The comedies of Chaplin. That kick of the heel and the walk down the road toward the horizon. History where it belongs. The high point of my book, *Configurations at Midnight*, is in one of the last stanzas: "Hamlet's shadows. Akhmatova's ghosts, / Old sorrows, what are old sorrows to me? / The arras is drawn, St. Petersburg survives."

Wallace Stevens sums up the right poetic attitude in his poem "The Man on the Dump." The poet lives in an ivory tower with a view of the city dump:

"One sits and beats an old tin can, lard pail. / One beats and beats for that which one believes . . . / Where was it one first heard of the truth? The the."

In your essay, "Witness Poetry," you write: "Belfast depends on prosody." You insist on the relationship between poetry and morality.

Poetry is a moral occupation. You can't lie in poetry. The minute you lie, you're insincere. You're hoodwinking yourself and somebody else and you're aware of it. Sir Philip Sidney says, "Of all liars, the poet is the least liar." Solzhenitsyn says the same thing in his Nobel acceptance speech. So does the novelist Faulkner. Ezra Pound, in his *Cantos*, demands "sandpiles for the children."

Your work has been criticized for being difficult, highly stylized. What is your response to this criticism?

That worries me very much. In the introduction to my book *Configurations at Midnight*, I define the structure of the poem. The last sentence in the foreword is: "The level of communication that is current was a problem." I was asked recently what I meant. Listen to talk on the TV any night and you have the answer: incoherence, pubescence, rambling and "you know." I am still waiting for adults who have grown up. Ten to one, those who are literate don't read poems.

"The moment is not only itself," you wrote somewhere in your poems.

The poem isn't written until it is read.

The resolution of the rich sense of process is something I especially admire in those poems of yours that have their locale here in your home in the Eastern Townships, the poems out of North Hatley. There is a simplicity, a directness, and a strong sense of a celebration of the world in these poems.

The moment, each moment, incorporates memory; you can't help that, it's the nature of the beast. And each moment incorporates a future since that brings in vision, brings in what is aimed at. Here, the countryside incorporates less irony, less violence, no need for sarcasm. The directness and simplicity is a resolution of life itself – life which nobody ultimately can answer, I suppose, unless you are very religious.

What part does religion play in your work?

A very heavy part. Not in any institutional sense: that Elijah went to heaven in a chariot or that the Virgin Mary physically went up to heaven, standing on a cloud, as the painters would have it. I read today that 69% of Americans believe in the existence of angels, that sort of nonsense, that the percentage of belief falls to 49% for devils. The discrepancy means hope, I suppose. Human respect for humans seems to me a much more effective activity than wings and ascension. I get impatient and indignant: Faith is an ignorance. Testing through suffering and mortality is unacceptable and blackmail. I don't light candles.

I am religious only by instinct, no matter how I try to attack the inborn conviction that I have to have God. There is no immediate answer to the question: "How did God come to be?" Milton's "Light." Pound's "Light." The book of Genesis' "Word." You picked up a book on my coffee table when you came in, to see what I was reading. The book is *The Mind of God: The Scientific Basis for a Rational World*, by the physicist Paul Davies. The author is atheist. So I search and attack and refer to God and religion in my poems. Of all my reading, I end up at a book by Robert Jastrow called *God and the Astronomers* which ends:

For the scientist who has lived by his faith in the power of reason, the story ends up like a bad dream. He has scaled the mountains of ignorance; he is about to conquer the highest peak; as he pulls himself over the final rock, he is greeted by a band of theologians who have been sitting there for centuries.

For the foreseeable future, I'll believe in poetry.

North Hatley, Quebec, December 30, 1991

GEORGE JOHNSTON

It is an hour's drive from Montreal along Highway 138 to Huntingdon and George Johnston's house. He is waiting for me in the doorway on this early Saturday morning in late December. George and Jeanne speak about their house, built at the turn of the century by the owner of the mill for one of his employees. The floors are an unusual alternation of maple and cherrywood. There is a small stained glass window on the stairs, and a pane of stained glass above the big front window. In the hallway there is a framed poem of P.K. Page's "Deaf-Mute in the Pear Tree," and a painting by bill bissett. We pass between two white pillars into the living room where a large bookcase extends to the ceiling; it contains old editions of English literature as well as history (the seven volumes of Edward Gibbon's *The Decline and Fall of the Roman Empire*), philosophy books and a generous music collection. On one shelf is a selection of current literary periodicals. There is a modern black piano in the dining room. A fine

Norwegian chair sits in the corner. George had asked that a tape recorder not be used since he thinks that it creates an artificial effect. He is an excellent conversationalist, with a strong sense of his audience, no doubt formed by his teaching Old and Middle English and Old Norse at Carleton for nearly thirty years. One is aware of the rhythm of his phrases; his speech has the resonant oral quality of his poetry.

*

We have heard much about Montreal's literary life during the twenties and thirties. What writers and critics were in Toronto when you were there as a student in the mid thirties?

To tell the truth, I was hardly aware of a literary life in Toronto, except at the university. There was one intellectual sort of magazine which came out once a month. It was more like a paper than a magazine. It was *Saturday Night*. It's still going, but it's not at all the same. It was edited by B.K. Sandwell then. It was a good paper. Except among my fellow undergraduates, I knew no writers at that time. I found my fellow undergraduates, however, quite influential.

George spoke of some of his fellow undergraduates who were critics and writers. He considered Roy

Daniells a "helpful instructor," "useful critically." The influential critic, Desmond Pacey, a year behind George, became a "cause célèbre" with a "serious objection" to a six line poem called "Annabelle." George formed an acquaintance with Margaret Avison who had commented briefly on a few of his poems. However, it was George's immediate peers with whom he interacted. He considered W.E. Finbow one of the more interesting poets, though he has not published since. Frances Russell, a very shy girl, and Jim Taylor were important figures. So was Bob McRae, Jeanne's brother, who later taught philosophy and published articles and books. Gordon Roper was an early influence on George, introducing him to the work of different writers, including a favourite of George's, A.E. Housman.

Jim Taylor was one of the most influential at that time. His story is a sad one. He became a Daughters of the British Empire scholar at Cambridge. He studied under Ludwig Wittgenstein, then went to California and got a PhD there. When the war broke out, he joined naval intelligence. But he was murdered in Australia after the war on his first night there. J.C., as we called him, longed to write poetry and was a very good reader. He knew when I had gone off the rails. He knew when I was doing well. I owe him a great debt for that.

George and Jim Taylor crossed the Atlantic as cattlemen and spent the summer of 1936, the year of the Berlin Olympics, bicycling around Germany. What signs of war did you see coming?

It was a militaristic society. Black shirts marching. Brown shirts marching. And also boys and girls marching. They were all organized in a military way. The Germans said, "Hitler doesn't want a war." We argued with them. It was obvious to us, at any rate. The Spanish Civil War broke out while we were in Belgium.

Did any of this find its way into your poetry?

No. The influential poets of the time that I was reading were W.B. Yeats, A.E. Housman, and T.S. Eliot. There was an intelligent, eccentric Irishman, a church organist, a remittance man I met. His name was Crookshank. He was called "Barney" because he was born on St. Barnabas Day. He was the one who put me onto reading Yeats because he had known Yeats in Dublin. I wrote a little poetry in high school, more in university. A high school poem was published in the old *Mail and Empire.* My university poems were published in the Victoria College literary journal *Acta Victoriana* and some comical and satirical poems were published anonymously in *The Varsity.*

You wrote short stories and novels before publishing your first book of poems. Why did you not continue with prose?

I did continue to write some prose. I had one short story published before the war in the *London Mercury.* It was picked up by an American magazine and published there. Then I wrote two novels. One was accepted by an agent in New York. After the war they asked did I want the manuscript back. And I said, "Destroy it." I have published a few short stories since the war.

Did you do any writing during the war?

The one poem, "The Cruising Auk." I kept composing bits of poetry, but I didn't keep any of them. I never really stopped composing poems since the satirical poems I wrote in high school.

Satire is one of your strengths.

It's not satire; it's rather comic irony. All the poems in the middle section of *The Cruising Auk* were a little world all their own. It's sort of a lyric world. It has comic irony, but also a lyrical tone.

One gets a strong sense of your knowledge of English literature in your poems.

I suppose that among the classic writers, the English classics, that is, one favourite was Alexander Pope. He was an important influence I think and rather a contrast, or a balance perhaps, to Yeats, Housman, and Eliot, and I suppose Wordsworth as well. I have always been a reader of Shakespeare and Chaucer. And there is more than a fair amount of influence from the King James version of the Bible, Old and New Testament. There are phrases and bits from the Bible, unacknowledged, even cadences.

When the war finished George went back to graduate school where Northrop Frye got him interested in

William Blake. George did his MA thesis on the visionary English poet under Frye's direction. In 1947 George got a teaching position in New Brunswick at Mount Allison University and recalls how financially tough times were, although they managed, he suggested, well enough. After two years at Mount Allison and another year as a graduate student in Toronto, George was lucky enough to be given a teaching position at Carleton. There were few openings then. At this time he was preparing for his work on his dissertation, the influence of Blake on Yeats. He spent a summer on Blake's Jerusalem; *when the academic year was over he returned to it, and discovered, to his dismay, that he recalled very little of what he had read. He remembered that his thesis director, Northrop Frye, had said that of course he would have to read Madame Blavatsky. When recalling this to me George raised his hand and said that he refused to read Madame Blavatsky. He told the chairman at Carleton that he wasn't going to complete his dissertation, and they could fire him if they wanted to. Of course, they didn't. George smiled and said perhaps there were enough PhDs in the world.*

Translation has been important to you as a scholar and a writer. I am intrigued as to why you began to translate Scandinavian literature.

My interest started when I was a graduate student after the war. I had been out for ten years after my BA. I went back to graduate school because I was married late in the war, and it was clear I wasn't going to make a living for two people, let alone myself, by writing. At that time there was little support for writers in Canada. There was no Canada Council. There was remarkably little publishing in Canada.

Your interest in Scandinavian literature began then.

I studied *Beowulf* under John Robins at Victoria College. That was graduate school, of course. And I was very enthusiastic about *Beowulf*, but I also read in translation two of the sagas: they were William Morris' translation of *The Saga of the Volsungs* and also Hight's *The Saga of Grettir the Strong*. And I made up my mind then that I would learn Old Icelandic at the first opportunity, which was not for another seven years, on my first sabbatical leave. I learned Old Icelandic from Peter Foote.

He was a key influence on you.

Yes. He taught me informally. We read several sagas that winter and then I suggested that we translate a saga together, and he agreed.

When did you first meet Peter Foote?

I wrote to University College in London, and said I wanted to study Old Norse. Peter Foote answered and invited me to come, when I got to England, and see him. In translating *The Saga of Gisli*, I discovered a major interest. I went on and translated *The Greenlanders' Saga* and *The Faroe Islanders' Saga*.

The Faroe Islands were an important discovery for you. You made four trips there, and translated a number of Faroese poets.

I went to Denmark on my second leave with my family. I wanted to read the Scandinavian languages because so much critical material about the saga literature is written in one or other of them. I thought if I learned Danish, as well as Icelandic, I'd have enough to work on. I already knew some German. And I learned Danish in Denmark. I realized it was the key to modern Scandinavian literature so far as I was concerned. We had met Hans and Else Bekker-Nielsen in Toronto when Hans was teaching there for two years. They found a house for us in Denmark and were very friendly. They talked us into going up to the Faroe Islands because they were so enthusiastic about them, and we agreed. I had already translated *The Faroe Islanders' Saga*. So then I learned Faroese.

What about the Faroe Islands appeals to you?

We made good friends there. I started translating two very fine poets, Christian Matras and Karsten Hoydal. *Poetry* [Chicago] published a few of my translations of Matras and Hoydal. I saw them both on our last trip, but they've died since.

You have a strong liking for Christian Matras' work.

It's hard to describe. It's very poetic. There is a haunting quality to his work. He loves the islands and the language. His rhythms are strong. I found him a very attractive person. I admired his handling of verse and the rhythms in which he writes about the islands, and his poems are humane, about people and friendships.

There is a relationship to your own work.

Yes. I think so. He's a poet I would naturally take to. Both he and Karsten.

Can you elaborate on the influence of translation on your own work?

The strongest influence is from the sagas. Not only the poetry. *The Saga of Gisli* has many poems in it. But also the prose of the sagas, and especially the rhythms, of both poetry and prose. The rhythms are almost more influential than anything. Another thing I think very important is that in translating the sagas I learned to become selective about my language. I chose, as far as possible, Germanic, or at any rate pre-Shakespearian words, especially for the saga translations.

You place importance on the knowledge of the language. You have said you spend a great deal of time with the OED.

I really want to know the background of the words I use. I want to know whether a word is English or not and how long it's been in use and what sort of overtones it has picked up in its history.

Do you find it possible to have that kind of purity in language today?

Of course there has been no such thing as a pure English since the Norman Conquest, or even before. You have to weed out a lot. But a language for poetry is still available in modern English. It's not quaint.

It doesn't need to be archaic. It's still current. But you have to dig it out from all the junk, from all the flashy words, and faddy words that English has taken on. I also feel that much technical language has no poetic value. I am interested in the syntax, that is, how words relate to one another. Translating forces you to get down to the exact relation of words. Because, for instance, the sagas use a very spare language, almost no description. It's all in the story. The sagas don't interpret motives. These appear in action and in speech. And before reading the sagas I had already become suspicious of adjectives and adverbs.

Like Pound in ABC ...

Pound, however, has had very little influence on me. I admired Pound, but for some reason he hasn't influenced me, whereas Eliot's rhythms, clearly, at one time did influence my poetry. The sagas have helped me a great deal.

I was struck by the ancient and modern qualities of the Faroese translations.

What really struck me, in the Faroese poetry, was the quality of the language. Christian Matras was interested in this. Their language is as interesting as Icelandic, though not their literature. Icelandic literature is one of the great literatures of Europe. And the Icelandic language must be the purest Germanic language in existence.

Faroese wasn't written down until the twentieth century.

That is how it has kept its purity for so long; it was a backwater, out of the way. The language was not written down; there was virtually no written Faroese before 1890. Danish was the official language of the islands. Faroese was spoken and sung, but its written literature is all modern. There were ballads, but these were only written down in the nineteenth and twentieth centuries. It's a comparatively unspoiled language. What I mean by that is, well, compare it with English. Ease of communication, especially in the twentieth century, between different kinds of English (American, British, Australian, South African) has resulted in the rapid development of a superficial English. Faroese seems unspoiled because words that express ordinary emotions have not yet been debased by widespread currency. English has become such a common language, a trading language, that many of its words that we might want to use no longer have purity of meaning, or poetic resonance.

At this point we broke for lunch. After a hearty continental lunch, we went for a walk to the post office. George spoke about the town having too many mediocre restaurants and a new pizzeria. He spoke about the traffic being bothersome, especially in the summer. He talked about moving from the old house at Cook's Lines because of age and convenience. Everywhere had to be driven to. Walking is an important ritual of his life. He is a strong walker, taking long brisk strides through the cold raw air. For George, walking is aligned to compo-

sition. He speaks about how sometimes the poems come quickly. But mostly not. A poem seldom takes less than a month. Some take years. And he speaks about how he composed the translations of the poems in the sagas on his walks in Ottawa between his house and his office at Carleton, a distance of about 2 1/2 miles. These eight-line poems took about a month each of such peripatetic composition. One listens to the rhythm and texture of his speech. He almost casts a spell the way he weaves words. One is aware of how close the words are to the things he is describing.

In their kitchen Jeanne shows me a delightful picture painted by a friend which has a tropical atmosphere; George is surrounded by the six children sitting on what seems like a huge yellow boat. There are several other pictures in the kitchen with colourful marble swirls done by their grandchildren. A concern with family and friends is seen in the Johnston home, and is reflected in George's poems, such as the much anthologized "Cathleen Sweeping," and in his later poems, which are dedicated to his friends. In the dining room, there is a Kawai piano and a songbook opened to "Nobody Knows the Trouble I've Seen." There is a portrait of George painted in 1938 by John MacPherson, when George was living on Ironbound, a small island seven miles from Peggy's Cove. There are three or four nesting Blackwood tables, a Chinese coffee table and vases from Jeanne's parents who were missionaries in China.

What poets do you reread?

George Herbert, Spenser, Coleridge, Wordsworth, Shakespeare, Donne. Edward Thomas is one I go back to. Hardy is one I go back to, and A.E. Housman and David Jones. I had a great go at Gerard Manley Hopkins, not to mention a few Canadian poets. There are a lot of poets I would go back to, but I spend so much time on Norse now.

At the beginning of your career the subjects of your poems were imaginary: Mr. Murple, Mrs. McGonigle and Aunt Beleek. Where did these characters come from?

They came out of the blue in my last year as an undergraduate.

One of my favourites is Mr. Murple.

It's obvious there's a whole lot of me in him (or at least I think there is), as well as the other characters. Anna Livia Plurabelle telescopes into Anabelle. I was reading *Anna Livia Plurabelle* at the time, the Faber paperback published before the war, part of what James Joyce called "Work in Progress," which ultimately became *Finnegans Wake*. Anna Livia Plurabelle was given to me by Barney Crookshank. These characters were very short lived. They started before the war, filled the middle section of *The Cruising Auk* and survived in two or three poems in my second book *Home Free*. The poem "Love in High Places" dismissed them. There were no imaginary characters after that. It was a mood I wasn't able to recapture. I wasn't sure I wanted to recapture it.

In Home Free *your poems turn more toward experience.*

In *The Cruising Auk* there were many poems based on my own experience. These were not ironic. In *Home Free* I could no longer be ironic in quite the same way. The irony was no longer as light-hearted as it had been. And partly I had emotional ties to my family, older and younger. They simply made a light-hearted irony impossible in poetry, but not necessarily in life. I became more serious about poetry itself. The shift is not a fundamental one. The seriousness was there already, even in the comic ironic poems.

In your poetry the emphasis is more on the poetry than the personality of the poet. It is the poem that is important.

Yes, I feel that very strongly. I think the poem should compose itself as far as possible. I do make certain demands of my own. One is that it should make some kind of sense, and take a recognizable shape. It should rhyme if I can persuade it to, but it need not say what I think I want it to say. I am willing to be surprised by what it ends up saying. I consider that however hard we try to connect the poem with the poet who wrote it, it does say its own say as if it were anonymous. I don't think that knowledge of the poet really helps the poem much. If it really is poetry, it detaches itself. It goes its own way. If you have to know the poet in order to understand the poem, then the poem lacks what I consider an almost essential quality, which is anonymity.

What one is immediately aware of in your work is the oral quality of it, that is, the rhythm and the sound. I am thinking of such poems as "War on the Periphery" and "Elaine in a Bikini."

I think it is very important to understand that when I speak about rhythm I am not meaning a jingle, although there are some pretty obvious and repetitive rhythms that are quite successful, quite profound. I think rhythm must be the most ancient element in poetry. In fact, the older forms of words in Indo-European are certainly rhythmical, but I think it has become hard for us to hear rhythms. I think the mechanical rhythms have dulled our capacity to hear primal rhythms, like the wash of the sea on the shore. Eliot mentions the beat of horses' hooves. And something that was part of my childhood and is gone now, was that most beautiful rhythm of sleigh bells. In a town they were an almost constant background of sound; you heard them against the silence that the snow imposed. I do think that there are certain natural rhythms one never tires of hearing, and some poets seem able to capture these, you know. It's hard now, because so many of them are gone from daily life.

Performance has been a key word in recent Canadian poetry. Yet performance is not new. Poetry has been performed for thousands of years: Homer, the Icelandic poets, the troubadours, Wordsworth, The Four Horsemen. Performance is important to you. You are one of the few Canadian poets who recites his work. One also thinks of bill bissett and Yvonne Trainer. Gwen MacEwen recited her poetry too.

I think there's a temptation in performing to rely on an easy or familiar manner, a wisecracking manner, to pretend that what you're reading is not rhythmical. I think that temptation has resulted in a lot of unremarkable poetry. I think poetry should be read with an awareness of the shape of the lines, where the ends come, and some awareness of stresses or at any rate the cadenced phrases, and in fact I think an almost chanted delivery, at least the suggestion of a chant, is most appropriate to poetry. There are some poets who do read that way. Al Purdy reads with an awareness of the rhythm of his poetry, and so do Jay Macpherson, James Reaney, Colleen Thibaudeau, John Newlove and some others. Poetry ought not to be read as if it is prose. It ought to have its own formality. And these poets whom I have mentioned are aware of this.

In the introduction to your Collected Poems *you speak of the importance of grammar and syntax. Do you think that modern poetry has lost touch with some of these elements?*

A knowledge of how an English sentence works or can work is something few contemporary Canadian poets have. Few of them take pleasure in balancing clauses or even producing a good narrative sentence using the co-ordinating conjunctions "and" and "but." This means that many of the resources of the language are not being used. On the other hand one hears frequent clumsy and repetitive clauses of a modifying nature, strung together by such conjunctions as "like" and "as."

The Lay of Thrym is one of your most recent translations. It is a powerful and dramatic poem.

It is an Eddic poem, anonymous of course, perhaps of the tenth century. It has a common Germanic form. It uses essentially the same metre as the Old English poems and *Beowulf*. It rhymes initial letters, a kind of rhyme that is known as alliteration. Its metre is based on lines, or half-lines, of two stressed syllables and usually two unstressed syllables, but occasionally more. In *The Lay of Thrym* the lines are paired, by means of alliteration; that is, the first letters of the two stressed syllables of the first line alliterate with the first letter of the first stressed syllable of the second line of the pair. This metre has a very strong rhythm. There are few particles. The words of the poems are nearly all nouns, pronouns, and verbs, which also produce a strong grammatical effect. I have used this sort of metre occasionally, modified somewhat, for many years. It seems to go very well in modern English.

What are you working on now?

I have had a poem written to me in French verse

by Robert Melançon. The only verse I've written in the past two years is an answer to it and perhaps this will develop into a correspondence. We would both be glad if it did. But what is current for me is the preparation of four sagas, in the hope of publication.

Huntingdon, Quebec, December 30, 1990

P.K. PAGE

It is a warm November afternoon as the bus winds down under the oak trees along Cadboro Bay Road; in the distance Cadboro Bay shines. I get off below the street where P.K. Page lives. There is a pathway through an arbour down to the water. Page lives in a comfortable residential area of Victoria. The sky is beginning to cloud over. Across the road a neighbour is digging up plants. As I walk up the steps toward the house surrounded by various plants and neat shrubs I am reminded of the rich garden that Page describes in her book, *Brazilian Journal*. There are not many flowers left. Page greets me warmly. I am struck by her articulation and the cheerful quality of her voice.

In the living room of her house I am immediately aware of the artwork. There are voices in the kitchen, and a radio playing quietly. The interview takes place in a wide ranch style room which reflects the countries where Page has lived. There are several books on the table where I place the tape recorder: *The*

Malaise of Modernity and *Sources of the Self: the Making of the Modern Identity* by Charles Taylor, and a current issue of *Scientific American*. On the chair opposite me I see *The Oxford Companion to the Mind*. On the far wall is a cityscape by Charles Comfort ... "before he became dour," P.K. says. There is a painting of a religious procession by a Brazilian named Benjamin. She points out two polychrome ceramic oxen from the Mexican village of Metepec which were made for a spring festival. At the right end of the bookcase is an Australian aboriginal bark painting. By the fireplace is a vase containing large artificial flowers from Mexico that recalls Al Purdy's poem about Page, "Great Flowers Bar the Roads." On the wall that leads to the basement is a large hanging of a winged two-horned horse-like creature designed by Leonora Carrington; in the hallway a print by Toni Onley. Down the hallway is Page's "unspeakably untidy study" with an entire wall of art supplies. On her desk is a copy of the poems of Anna Akhmatova. In the guest room is a peacock mask given to her by Constance Rooke. There is also the original of the "Stairwell" reproduced in *Brazilian Journal*.

*

Do you remember the time that you decided to write?

I don't. A lot of writers say things like, "There I

sat on the living room floor and suddenly I realized I was going to be a poet." But it never came to me in a blinding flash. I grew up in a family where family members recited. I don't mean formal recitations. Mother had a memory for verse and when anything was appropriate, she would spout it. She remembered a great deal of Shakespeare and the Romantics. She also had a memory for jingles and nonsense rhymes, as had my father. I mainly remember the rhythms. I think they had something to do with why I wrote. Then, of course, once that tremendous release of hormones starts, you have all that wild energy that you don't know what to do with.

Your parents were from a different culture. Did that affect you?

I am sure it affected me. I grew up with an English accent in the Canadian Midwest, so I got teased a lot. I don't think the fact that my parents were English affected me as much as that they were very free spirits. At a time when everybody went to church, they didn't. I was never taken to church or sent to Sunday school. I didn't do all the things nice little girls did. My parents weren't conformists. They didn't end up in jail or the lunatic asylum, so they conformed to some extent. *[Laughter.]* But they weren't run of the mill, either. One part of me liked it and one part of me hated it. It made me too different.

You had connections with several literary magazines in the 1940s: Preview, First Statement, CV, *and*

Northern Review. *These magazines had quite different orientations, yet you were able to relate to them all.*

Well, I wonder if we thought about the differences at that time? You may, from this vantage point, see differences in the magazines. You have a revisionist position, whether you want to or not.

Certainly. James Reaney said the same thing. He didn't see aesthetics in the same way we see it today.

I think that's true. There wasn't so much analysis about it all. What we were primarily concerned with was having somewhere to get work published. There was almost nowhere that published poetry. But there was certainly a difference between *First Statement* and *Preview*. John Sutherland's rejection by *Preview* led him to start *First Statement.* Also his stance was passionately nationalist, whereas *Preview*'s wasn't. *Preview* had been started by Patrick Anderson who, at the time, had communist sympathies. The rest of us were variously leftward leaning.

Is that what you see as the main difference between those two groups?

I think so. John never wanted to publish anyone who wasn't Canadian whereas, in theory, we would have published anyone we thought good. In practise, we were so anxious to get our own stuff in print *[laughter]* there was rarely room for anybody else.

You said before that you were influenced by Patrick Anderson.

I don't know how much my thought was influenced by Patrick, but my work was, even though I am not a mad admirer of his work.

Were there particular things that you were aware of in the style that you liked about his work?

The rush of images seemed extraordinary to me. I hadn't read a great deal of modern poetry when I met the *Preview* group. I had read Eliot who was a spare writer, really. Patrick was writing more like Dylan Thomas or George Barker, whom I had not then read. He was the first poet, for me, who indulged in such a spill of images.

Was there an influence of the socialists and W.H. Auden, Spender, MacNeice, C. Day Lewis?

Yes, considerable. Until I met the *Preview* group I hadn't read any of them. But once I did it was natural for me to align myself with their point of view. Because I had always been pro "underdog" this was a natural slot waiting for me to fall into.

In some ways those poems seem politically engagées. There is a political sense to them, more so than in your later work. Would you see it that way?

I think there's very little political sense to my later work although I don't think my point of view has changed essentially. My sympathies are still the same but I don't find myself writing that way now. There's been a shift of direction, but not a denial.

You've talked in the past about the influence of

Sutherland and Anderson. What about the other members of Preview?

I don't think Sutherland influenced me at all, although I had known him a long time pre-*Preview*. As to Klein, although it seems remarkably arrogant to say so, I think maybe I had an influence on Klein. Somewhere he has said that Patrick and I both influenced him. What I caught from Patrick, he caught from us both. His work changed during the *Preview* period.

What kind of a figure was A.M. Klein?

He was a darling. I loved him. Actually he was only nine years older than I but he seemed to belong to a different generation. This had to do with a series of things, I think, with the fact that he was married, had children, and a law practice. He was already established as a poet and in a career. Although God knows what sort of a career his law practice was! His partner must have gone mad. What I didn't know at the time is that he was very hard up, so he could only afford one suit and it had to be the suit in which he could appear as a respectable lawyer. The rest of us were in whatever was the equivalent of jeans. Jeans were not on the market then, but whatever the casual clothing was, Klein didn't wear it. He wore a tie and his navy blue suit. He had thick glasses so you didn't see his eyes very well, but the way the light caught the lenses made him look as if he was twinkling all the time. And he was one of the funniest men you could possibly imagine. It was a treat to be with him because he was so quick. So witty. I find him a wonderful poet and can't think why people today don't see it. But they will again. For the moment he is out of fashion. I love his wit and the sound of his language and the lushness of his imagery, and the fact of his being Jewish introduced a new note into Canadian poetry: the description of his sisters making themselves beautiful ...

The mirroring sisters in "Autobiographical"...

Yes. Yes. Yes. Oh, he was a treat, Klein, a darling. Fun to be with.

Did you get together often?

Well, we got together for meetings once he joined *Preview*, which wasn't at the beginning. And then I used to see him occasionally. We would sometimes go to the bar of the Mount Royal Hotel and have one drink each. And we'd read our latest poems to each other – aloud – to the startled surprise of the waiter because Klein couldn't read *sotto voce*. He had a great declamatory tone.

Wartime was difficult for the people at home in Canada. In your poems, such as "The Stenographers" and "Election Day," you are concerned with that. Can you recall some of the difficulties of the period?

I suppose the major difficulty was the heartbreak of being on the edge of heartbreak all the time, because most women had men overseas or likely to go overseas. I had a father and a brother overseas. There's a great deal of anxiety in a situation like that. You never know from day to day whether you are going to hear that they are dead. Death was always in the air. It gave a very sharp edge to life.

On the home front, but at a lesser level, war meant rationing, something we had not encountered before. To go from the 1990s to rationing would be much more extreme than going from pre-war to rationing, because we were not such an affluent society then. We hadn't been spoiled rotten by being able to get strawberries out of season *[laughter]* and all the gourmet foods available today, but it did impose an air of restraint on people who were not financially poor. I am not talking about myself in this instance because, goodness knows, I was making all of eighty dollars a month! *[Laughter.]* Even the rich couldn't get as much sugar as they wanted or as much whiskey or tea without resorting to the black market. The other memorable thing was snow clearance in Montreal, or lack of it. As most able-bodied men were in the services, the streets were rarely cleaned and icier than you can imagine. It was almost impossible to walk sometimes. Snow piled up. And when they did clear the streets, they hadn't the equipment to haul it away, so there were high snow walls along Sherbrooke Street, for instance, that made the street a kind of tunnel. And when the *calèches* went by with jingling bells, you might have been in a Russian novel or so it felt to me, because I was reading the Russians at the time.

George Johnston said one of the rhythms that we no longer hear is the rhythm of sleigh bells.

That's true. And the horse. Wonderful sound, wonderful sound.

Did the war have a lasting effect on your work?

I don't know. Everything that happens to us has an effect. I'm not sure the First War didn't have an effect on me too, but not a conscious effect because I was too young. I was born during World War I and my father was fighting in the trenches. My mother was in a state of anxiety all the time, naturally, and I'm not sure this didn't come through the placenta *[light laughter]* into my very bones. I can remember as an adolescent going to the movies and if they had anything to do with war they gave me the absolute willies. I covered my eyes and behaved in a way different from my contemporaries. So I don't know. I suspect that in certain ways we are more sensitive than we know we are. In others, we are astonishingly obtuse.

Some of your early poems are about children and adolescents.

"Young Girls," "Sisters," "Only Child." Yes, I wrote a lot about children. That was a period when I rarely wrote about myself. Usually people start by writing about themselves because they haven't anything else to write about, and then they look up and write about the outside world. I seem to have gone the other way. When I was young I was observing all the time. It is only now that I am more personal. Perhaps the confessional poets affected me.

So you appreciate an objective poetry as opposed to a poetry in the self or of the self.

What do you mean by objective? Eliot's "objective correlative" had a great deal of meaning for me, and it still has. If you can find the correct "correlative," it seems to me that you can make what might have been only personal into something more universal.

And yet, later on in your life, you used the "I."

The many eyes within the "I." "The brain is a crowd." It is. We have everything in us, I think, all of evolution.

Do you see your work as going through several phases? I am borrowing the word "phase" from one of the essays you wrote.

I suppose it has. It's different now from my first published work. But there are many recurring themes. Anyone looking at it closely would see many of the same things simply wearing a different dress.

Is there a time in your life when something changes, when you write a poem like "Stories of Snow"?

I am not sure I understand the question. Did something in me change when I wrote "Stories of Snow"? How can I see so far back? It's a pretty early poem. Maybe I took a giant step with it. I may not have written anything better. Funny, the fact that you don't, in a sense, progress.

It's a hard poem for me to get a handle on.

The end of the poem baffled me when I wrote it. In fact, I only understood what I was saying a few years ago. Occasionally one writes beyond oneself or beyond one's conscious knowledge. Different selves quite possibly write different poems.

Your first move from Canada was to Australia. What kind of an effect did Australia have on you?

I loved it, contrary to the prophecies of my friends who told me I would hate it. Seeing different constellations in the night sky was very heady. Flora and fauna were fabulous. My eye is a very active organ and Australia gave it plenty of exercise. In addition there was the change of lifestyle to a much more formal, structured way of life.

In Brazil, you said you learned another language. And, you wrote that you learned to see differently. Yet, you didn't write much poetry in Brazil.

Learning another language may have had something to do with not being able to write. I wasn't hearing my own speech rhythms. I tried to write, God knows. I stared at endless pages of emptiness. And although I thought I wasn't writing, I was actually writing *Brazilian Journal*, which is a kind of poem. It's full of images. To compensate perhaps for no poetry I began to draw. All my life I have been interested in art. My earliest pocket money went on books of paintings rather than poetry. Many of my friends were painters, so the attempt to draw and paint fed whatever was needing to be fed, the part that writing poetry would have fed, had I been writing.

So it wasn't really silence, then.

No, it didn't feel like a silence.

Rilke has interesting things to say about silence. It took him ten years to write the Duino Elegies. *There were long periods before the outburst of the poems.*

Somewhere he says: " . . . one's left with a mere intimation of the kind of speech that may be possible *there*, where silence reigns." I think I sense what he is talking about. I don't think speech is the highest form of evolution. It is very necessary, not the highest.

Is silence important in your own work?

I think I understand meditators when they talk about silence, although I don't meditate. That is what the last lines of "Stories of Snow" are all about, "through to the area behind the eyes / where silent, unrefractive whiteness lies." I suspect that is the same silence.

You wrote, "The question of the mask confronted me with such violence in Mexico." The idea of the mask, then, was important to you at the time.

I had by then had about ten years of being an ambassador's wife, which was a masquerade for me. And the mask was pretty much like Rilke's in the *Notebooks of Malte Laurids Brigge,* bound on by all those lengths of silk. The more I tugged, the firmer it stuck. My psyche had had just as much as it could bear. It was a difficult period for me, although I was very interested in Mexico. But that role, I had never been in love with it to begin with. I could play it, but it was not where my interests lay. At the end of ten or twelve years I had had enough.

The sense of the other that's in "Arras," you said you become someone else, or "the other," important to you. I think of the persona, Melanie, when you write in a different voice.

"Cullen" is an early example of another voice. And "Man with One Small Hand." It's easy for me to identify with other people, too easy. My work began by identifying with others. In some cases the characters of whom I wrote were totally fictitious.

What I am interested in is the fact that you are open to so many different kinds of writers across the scale, different periods and different cultures.

The mystical poets of the Middle East had an effect on me, no question about that. Rumi, fabulous, extraordinary man, helped make me aware of a range of ideas, some of which are unknown in this culture. Interesting how the poetry from different ages, different cultures, offers us elements our own culture may have lost completely, for good or bad. We are all so blinkered by our own upbringing, locked in. Other literatures help us to see differently. I was both amused and irritated to read the blurb about me in the new Harcourt Brace Jovanovich anthology which said that I had been influenced by Sufi ideas, and that Sufism is a Muslim sect whose members turn their backs on the world in order to find unity with God. It is utterly absurd. Perhaps there is a Muslim sect that calls itself Sufic, but the statement as it stands is as if one were to say that Christianity is a sect of the Salvation Army. It is as distorted as that. And as for turning one's back on the world, I think my reading in this area has, if anything, freed me to immerse myself more in the world than is my natural bent.

What about other poets – W.B. Yeats, Blake and Rilke?

They are all poets I have loved and read, especially Rilke. Blake and Yeats were and are always there. Younger, I was not altogether sympathetic to Rilke's angels, but lately I have come to terms with them.

Are you talking about the Duino Elegies?

I can remember reading the *Duino Elegies* on the streetcar going to work and finding myself in the barns, having totally forgotten to get off. *[Laughter.]* Wonderful poems. Extraordinary poems. I am still very moved by the Spender/Leishman translation even though I find myself thinking this new guy,

Stephen Mitchell, is very, very wonderful, maybe better. But the first translation is like your first love. It always has a special significance for you.

I wrote a poem about Rilke.

Did you? I've written a *glosa*. Do you know what a *glosa* is?

No.

It's an early fifteenth century Spanish form. You choose four lines from another poet and then you write four ten-line stanzas, each ending with one of the borrowed lines, taken in order. There is a rhyme-scheme involved too: The sixth and ninth lines have to rhyme with the stolen tenth. I thought what I would do was take lines from all the poets I have really loved and pay a kind of homage to them by writing *glosas*. I've done five.

Who are the five?

Seferis, Wallace Stevens, Elizabeth Bishop, Auden, Rilke. I had a devil of a time finding four lines in Rilke that were not enjambed. It is very difficult, if not impossible, to use enjambed lines. I have still not found the right four lines from Yeats or Dylan Thomas. But I go on looking.

I'd like to turn to questions on writing. How does a poem begin for you?

I suppose there are two ways a poem can begin: by hearing a rhythm in my head, a very specific rhythm without words, which I put down in a sort of shorthand and then try to find words for; or by being "given" (who is the giver?) an image or a phrase that seems to contain the seeds of the poem. If neither happens, I don't write. I can't just sit down and say, "I'm going to write a poem about this, that or the other." Although that isn't entirely true, because as I get older I find that, after a fashion, I can.

In "Personal Landscape" perception is related to the heart, "the valvular heart's field glasses." The image reminds me of Margaret Avison's "optic heart" in "Snow."

Which came first? Her poem or mine?

When was yours written?

I don't know. A long time ago, in the early 1940s. And it doesn't matter. It reminds me that some years ago someone wrote a paper in which she showed how Atwood had influenced me. I had to write them and say, if influence there *was*, and I doubted it, it would have to be the other way round, because I was there first, by twenty-odd years. Certainly Atwood and I have used similar images, and because she has such a high profile it looks as if she has always been there, ergo, *she* must have influenced *me*. I don't know how much I believe in influence, anyway. Is it not more that certain people share a way of seeing? I realize that to some extent this contradicts what I said about Patrick Anderson. In fact, as I think about the subject, there seems suddenly a great deal to say. It is as if certain poets help you to see your own possibilities. Do you know the study of how songbirds learn to sing? A researcher reared some birds, all of the same species, singly, and in isolation. Each bird tried very hard to sing and finally managed to produce a recognizable but incomplete version of the song of its species. Only then was it allowed to hear the song of other birds, not of its own species and, from the songs heard, it selected the notes and rhythms necessary to produce its own species' song. Is this not perhaps what happens to us as poets, discovering our own voices?

Your vision is very much tied to the heart and not a literal way of looking at things; there's a strong emotional source for that.

I am very aware of the heart's physical location in my body. It may not actually be where I think it is, but I could draw its outline on my own torso. It is my feeling centre. Some people tell me they feel in their stomachs or heads or ...

You've written about the poet as conjuror. How important is magic for you?

The idea of the conjuror is attractive to me. Both my parents had a certain sleight of hand. They didn't develop it, only used it to amuse themselves and each other. As children, whenever magicians came to town we were always taken to see them. I loved the beauty of it, and the skill too, now that I am older and know it is a skill. And I love the idea of the unreliability of the senses. We get so locked into believing our senses that anything that can shake that a bit and bring the edifice down is useful.

My father was into that kind of thing. He was always telling riddles and playing tricks. He was always trying these out on us.

I love it. I grew up with it and I miss the playfulness. We have become a very unplayful people – turned sodden by TV, by observing. That's one of the reasons I love words. You can play with them.

Joyce said that he was never more serious than when he was playing.

All you have to do is watch children at play to know how serious it is.

There are certain times when a poem happens, when you get out of yourself and you get to a mode where you have a lot of freedom and that other mode takes over. And that's magical, I think. You get a kind of leap there.

Leaping Poetry by Robert Bly. Do you know it? It is a very fascinating little book. It is about the three brains (as distinct from the two hemispheres): the dinosaur or reptile brain, the mammalian brain and the neo-cortex, or new brain. Acupuncture is, I believe, connected to these three brains. Bly talks about the poetry that jumps from one brain to another. He thinks that in much good poetry there are these enormous leaps back and forth between the three brains.

He cites Rilke as being a poet of the neo-cortex, or visionary brain, and claims that most poets are writers of the mammalian, or emotional brain – and no bad thing, that! The reptile or dinosaur brain, the fight or flight (and eat!) is the Bush brain. *[Laughter.]*

Good.

Bly provides a little anthology of poems that he considers leap. I like the idea, I suppose, because I'm inclined to agree. You change gears without even knowing you are doing it.

Dreams are a significant part of your work. Many of them are located in bed and involve the dreaming or transformation of the speaker. As well, you mentioned the psychologist, Jung. Do you think dreams are intimately related to the development of the poem and the poet?

I don't know, Laurence. Certainly I have dreamed a lot or perhaps I should say that I've remembered many of my dreams. Once upon a time I was into heavy dreaming. *[Laughter.]* "Another Space" was based on a dream. I dreamed those people on the sand, dreamed of being reeled in like a fish by them. I couldn't catch all the overtones of the dream in a poem. Language won't do that. In "Unless the Eye Catch Fire" I no longer know which parts are dream and which I made up. The central image of seeing a spectrum beyond the normal was dreamed. A lot of my so-called ideas or images have come from dreams. I don't dream as much now, but I don't write as much either. I think there must be some quite strong link between the dreamer and the poet or between this dreamer and this poet, at any rate. "Cry Ararat!" was based on a dream, the dream of flying, which most of us have.

Recently I had a dream about visiting Northrop Frye's house.

Did you?

Last week, when I went to Moncton, I checked into a bed and breakfast. I was wearing my Northrop Frye sweatshirt and the woman said that Northrop Frye learned his music from Dr. Ross in the room that we were sitting in.

I love it when that happens. Ah, how interesting.

It's also interesting how dreams provide wonderful equivalencies or analogies to experience. They can't be put in any other way, a higher kind of logic.

That's right. And so the shorthand – written in shorthand, no, more – painted in shorthand. Yes. It's a parallel existence, perhaps.

There must be an area of the brain too, where the poets, the surrealists, W.B. Yeats with his automatic writing, tapped into that dreamlike area.

The collective unconscious. There's so much we don't know about, whole dimensions that we only get a taste of now and again which are just as real, if not more real, than this material one. Sometimes through writing one is able to get a glimpse of some of them.

Can you talk about a relation between painting and writing?

I've always felt it was the same pen, almost literally. I like a hard point to draw with. In actuality, I don't write with a pen or even a pencil, anymore. I write on a word processor. Nevertheless when I *do* write by hand, it's with a hard point, and many of my drawings are hieroglyphic. So there's an overlap between the two activities. When a certain stage is reached in drawing, there is a rhythm involved, which is not unlike the rhythm of writing a poem. And that is part of it, part of the pleasure of it. In drawing, of course, you don't get the play of words that you get with poetry, but in painting you get the additional succulence of colour.

In the video "Still Waters," you said you felt that you were a religious person, but not in the conventional sense. You said that you celebrate in terms of love and nature.

Did I? Perhaps I should never say anything, including this, because when I hear what I've said, I rarely agree! Today, I probably wouldn't use the word "religious" about myself. A religion is a belief system, isn't it? And anything can *become* a religion. *(I'm going to turn on the light.)* Although I have no system I believe in, I do have a sense of the divine, the other, the cosmological world, a sense only. Religions, I suppose, are believed to be routes to that.

You said that man was in danger in his relationship to nature, a danger more crucial than war. Do you remember what you meant by that?

So long as we don't use the bomb, and it looks as if we won't, a war cannot destroy the whole planet, but what we are doing environmentally could. We can destroy the air and the waters and the ozone layer. The realization of this comes over me very acutely from time to time, luckily not all the time, or I'd go crazy. But when I do remember I wonder why we are not all working in the service of the planet, full time. It was for this reason that, when asked to deliver the convocation address at Simon Fraser, I wrote a polemical poem. Don't think I don't ask myself whether a poet should be writing polemics. I do. All my life I have been opposed to polemical poetry. But times have changed. And I wonder.

Wallace Stevens talks about the great poem coming out of the earth, the epic of the earth.

The great poem. A purely polemical poem is not likely to be that. A great poet could probably do it. I think we are in very serious danger, but it's as if most of us are asleep to the possibility.

How do we wake up?

How do we wake up? How does the waker awake the sleeper? How does the sleeper awake the sleeper?

Thunder. [A sudden clap of thunder.]

That's rare here. You're conjuring up gods that we don't normally have. *[Laughter.]* It's not thundery country, this . . .

It's all around.

Yes. Maybe we're being shelled.

Victoria, British Columbia, November 8, 1992

FRED COGSWELL

The first part of this interview is conducted at the Fredericton Public Library on June 28, 2000. The second part, that concerns translation, takes place at Fred Cogswell's bungalow in Douglas, New Brunswick on June 4, 2002. We drive across the Fredericton bridge on a hot afternoon in late June. Adele, Fred's third wife, mentions that the house where Charles G.D. Roberts was born is for sale. The highway winds along the Nashwaak River. We stop at the mailbox at the corner of Island View. Fred takes out a letter from Tom Wayman. The flower garden is slightly overgrown and there is a bird bath in the centre of intersecting diagonal paths. It is a garden rich in a variety of flowers: roses, irises, poppies, junipers and spirea.

Fred keeps many of his books in his garage. We pass among the bric-a-brac of machinery, a gas lawn mower, and an old mattress leaning up against the books. I notice books by Wallace Stevens, Landor, Galsworthy's *The Forsyte Saga*, David Walker's *Harry Black* and a number of old Fiddlehead Poetry Books.

The living room is divided. On the garden side is a portrait of Fred by Gail Fox, his second wife, and a landscape of the Tantramar Marshes. There is a video collection which includes such works as *Amadeus*, *The Red Violin* (which he has recently watched) and Kenneth Branagh's *Hamlet*. There is a photo of Gail Fox's son, a photo of Fred taken at his own MA graduation, and a photo of him in his fifties standing on a dock in St. Andrews. On the window ledge there is a series of poetry books and a picture of an aboriginal chief.

Fred shows me a series of Fiddlehead Poetry Books, of which he has published over three hundred: *Earth Aches* by Robert Gibbs, *Mantle* by Sunyata MacLean, *Music for Moderns* by Linda Rogers, *From the Inside* by Heather Spears, *Kindling* by Leona Gom, *Lettre à Montréal* by Étienne Gérard, and *La Tempête du Pollen* by Huguette Légaré.

The interview takes place at Fred's kitchen table.

*

What was your family's background?

The background was largely, I think, of longevity on the part of the men in the family. On my father's side, ten generations take you back to the middle of the sixteenth century. The family originally was named after Coggesholle, of Essex, north of London. My family was in the wool business, so the Westbury Leigh section of the family lived in the western Downs of Wiltshire. After the wool business was established, a branch of the family moved to London. My first American ancestor, William, when he saw the Civil War coming, bought Sir Walter Raleigh's ship, the *Angel Gabriel*, and sailed to America, but was shipwrecked off the coast of Maine in 1635.

Not an auspicious beginning.

There were only two of these pilgrim ships that didn't make it safely; his was one of the two. One of the passengers on the *Angel Gabriel* was a young man named Bailey. This fellow was so frightened by the trip that he would not go back to England. He wrote such alarming tales of the journey that his wife would not travel to America to join him. If he hadn't brought his little boy along with him there would have been no Alfie Bailey in Canada.

What exposure to literature did you have while you were growing up?

I had considerable exposure while I was growing up because my father loved reading. We read any books that we could get our hands on in the family. I read many dictionaries. I read the *Anglo-Saxon Chronicle*, various great battles of history, the Old Testament and the New Testament. I read all the novels I could find. I read poetry. I read anything for ages and ages. When I went to high school, I discovered in the library the various classics of the 18th and 19th centuries, so I read them as well. I did a lot of reading. I also did a lot of mathematics because I was left to my own devices pretty well. What we had at that time in Centreville were grades 7-11 in the same room, with about sixty students. The teacher, who became principal of Fredericton High School, later died of Alzheimer's disease. He used to walk up and down the aisles and bang the students over the head, repeating, "Let that sink in." *[Laughter.]*

What was high school like for you?

I was happy because much of the time I was roaming around. I collected butterflies and moths. I studied birds. I also worked hard on the farm because I had chores to do. I walked over two miles to and from school and then, after my chores were done, I could run and play basketball sometimes. I was probably the top or next to the top student. I could have been the top student all the time, but I spent a lot of time playing basketball, baseball and various other sports.

When did you decide to become a poet?

Well, when I was about twelve, we were taking Palgrave's *Golden Treasury Book II*. I was in grade seven or thereabouts, so it was sort of a substitute for girls. If you don't have any money and you have sticking out teeth, and you can't pronounce words very well, you have social handicaps, money being the biggest. So what happened is that I took up reading dictionaries and encyclopaedias. I liked them. And I took up doing math. I used to be able to add thirteen and fourteen columns at once in my head, relationships which I now see helped my memory more than they helped my understanding.

You did your doctorate in Edinburgh. What kind of influence did this have on your thinking?

It didn't have very much influence. What I was working on was the concept of America in English Literature of the Romantic movement. I had to begin in the sixteenth century, and work my way through almost everything I could find in English literature until about 1834, the passing of the Reform Bill, and I came up with two notions. One was the idea that the British had of the aborigines in America, you know, the New World bits; and the other idea was the business of people coming from Europe to make a new start. Their polarities embraced romanticism and realism, and formed the messy alliance upon which much modern thought is based.

One can't talk about the development of English literature in New Brunswick without talking about Alfred G. Bailey. You were a good friend of his. Could you talk about Alfred G. Bailey and his founding of the Bliss Carman Society and The Fiddlehead?

The Fiddlehead was founded by Bailey around 1940. It was an ambition of his. Bailey was very conscious of ancestry, which was one of the things that we had in common. Our ancestors came from England on the same boat and we're related to the same kind of people, you know, like Emerson.

Do you remember your first meeting with Bailey?

Oh, yes, very well. I took freshman English from him. And I got on extremely well with Bailey. I was one of his star pupils. The thing about Bailey is that when he was younger he was called "hot lips Bailey." He could do things like the rhumba and the Charleston. He was also a would-be romantic poet who wrote lines like, "Dear face I love beside the blue Saint John / Your memory lingers on and on." But he went to the University of Toronto and the University of London and discovered modern poetry and all that stuff changed, you see.

Could you talk about the Bliss Carman Society?

Yes. The Bliss Carman Society was one of Bailey's pet ideas, for people who were interested in developing their poetry. To develop one's poetry one started out with what one had and then one gradually added to it the kind of things that were being done in one's own time. There was the notion of having a gap, but that you narrowed the gap gradually in your poetry. As a rule there were about a dozen members in the society.

Did Bailey introduce you to people like T.S. Eliot and Pound?

Those are the people that captured his interest.

Did those writers have an influence on you?

They had some influence on me. Some of it was deleterious and some of it wasn't. What I didn't like was that they were afraid of feeling. Since they were afraid of feeling they downplayed all positive feeling and went in for negative feeling, a kind of intellectual despair, particularly Pound and Eliot. Yeats and Dylan Thomas were better in this respect. I found myself liking people like A.E. Housman, even though Housman was of another tradition.

How was The Fiddlehead *founded?*

In 1945 The Bliss Carman society was made up of people who had been members for quite some time and they decided to produce a magazine. They printed this mimeographed magazine, a literary magazine, which had just the poetry of the members and all the members would have to agree to the poems. You couldn't get anything published unless it was approved by all the members.

Who was in that group?

There was the musician, Robin Bailey. I never met him because he graduated just a year before I came in 1945. Elizabeth Brewster was a senior in 1944 or 45. She was one of the best of them. Marg Cunningham was one of these members. Donald Gammon was a librarian. And his wife, Francis Firth, who was Bailey's assistant for a long time at the University of New Brunswick, was a member. Lyndon Peebles was also a member.

The painting by Bruno Bobak, in the English Department at the University of New Brunswick, portrays Robert Gibbs, Desmond Pacey, Kent Thomson, Allan Donaldson, Alden Nowlan and yourself. What was it like being in a department with so many writers?

It was better than it was at Sir George Williams (now Concordia University). The year I was at Sir George Williams they had people at McGill and Sir George Williams who ought to have talked to one another, but most refused to do so. Margaret Atwood, George Bowering, Clark Blaise, and Louis Dudek were all there, but they were a strange lot, in a sense. At UNB some members of *The Fiddlehead* were professors. Bailey was one. Pacey was another. They both participated in all the meetings and they were both very good people to have doing that. Without throwing too much weight around, they kept charge of things and used a considerable degree of tact. It was pretty harmonious, but it also caused you to become self-consciously critical whenever you took an extreme position.

Can you talk about Nowlan's presence and his contributions?

Alden Nowlan didn't show up on the scene until long after that. There was the Nowlan who had to express himself when he wasn't writing, by being social and by bringing to life fantasies like The Flat

Earth Society and the Stuart claimants to the British crown. What that was connected with to a certain degree was alcohol, parties, and men, men's parties because women were not very welcome. The Nowlan who wrote when he was sober showed very good treatment of women in his work. In it there is thought, sensuality, everything you would want in poetry. His poetry was accessible. You didn't have to know umpteen classical references to get the poems. He became slightly more abstract later on, but he didn't lose the basic qualities which I think are found in what are some of the finest poems ever written in Canada, for example, the one that he wrote about the retarded woman, her affection and his embarrassing self-consciousness.

So you see him as being one of the best Canadian poets?

Yes, he was a very fine Canadian poet. I have no doubt about that. He discarded his original use of rhyme and metrics. He didn't lose anything because he kept all of the essentials of poetry, the use of repetition with variation. He knew how to modulate and he did it very well. He had the habit, in life, of saying something exactly in such a way as to make it seem convincing.

Robert Gibbs has observed that some of your work is traditional in the forms that you use, for example, the epigram, the ballad and the lyric. Why have you chosen more traditional forms, rather than using contemporary forms that many Canadian poets use?

Because they required qualities and a discipline that were not necessarily being used much at the time, and I felt that they should be used. There was also the Chinese, the Taoist and the Japanese haiku. Twentieth-century English poetry was too barbarous to use these.

Northrop Frye said your early poems have the quality of vignettes. They express various forms of repression and violence in the characters of rural life. How much did they reflect the society you grew up in?

They were part of the society I grew up in. I despised them to some degree, but I did not say what was not true about the people concerned. There were real people behind everything I wrote. For example, the man who was a deacon in the Baptist church shot his neighbour, mistaking him for a groundhog. This did happen, you know. I went to school with this boy, Lefty. Only it was not hens, it was pigeons whose wings he nailed to the wall. He was, I believe, in revolt from his family's religiosity.

In the poem "New Brunswick," you write, "And all our beauty is our stubborn strength." What do you mean by this line?

What I mean by this is that there were codes of living, very rigorously marked. The code that was expected of a man was that a man did not complain; he showed courage and kept his troubles to himself.

Hardness and self-control were qualities a man should aspire to. Women had different qualities, not hardness, but softness, and such a thing called, I suppose, beauty. I did notice these particular divisions because everywhere that you went the women wound up in the parlour, the living room or the kitchen, and the men usually wound up in the stable. They all talked about what they were interested in, but the two interests did not come together any more than male and female came together within nature, except in times of mating. They were like different entities and, of course, women as students were not at all like men as students. The women were not expected to say anything. They were expected to agree with things, to write what they had memorized about what the teachers had said.

Your poems are often philosophical, evoking certain ethical problems. You are working out of a dialogue in the poem. You quoted W.B. Yeats, that out of the quarrel with the self, the poet produces poetry. Could you comment on the philosophical nature of your poetry?

The particular philosophical nature of poetry is that its function is to illustrate the qualities of the human mind that are the basis for the attitudes we have as human beings. Keep going farther than you've already gone, or you become a victim of what you've written up until that moment. In other words, you have to keep working. If you don't keep working your muscles get soft and you can get into a place where you are hardly strong enough to get yourself out of.

Fred, you have a talent for translation. How did you first become interested in translating?

I began to feel when I was reading, for example, *The Aeneid*, a passage like, "There are tears for misfortunes and mortal affairs touch the heart," had a meaning for me in my own language, as well as in the Latin language. The two things reinforced each other. Every so often that kind of thing would happen in something which I had read in translation.

You are related to the Girouards.

They came to Acadia from Poitou in about 1648 or 1649. My great-grandfather, who I think was called "Petit" Girouard, was the first Acadian MP. He died very young, when he was thirty-nine, of tuberculosis, leaving a family. He was married to a woman named Sophie Baker, who was about six feet two, I gather. Her father, after whom Baker Brook and Baker Lake in the County of Madawaska are named, kicked up quite a lot of trouble.

Did descending from an Acadian family have any influence on your translation?

It had some influence on my desire to know French. If I had been taught French, I would have spoken French properly, but my relatives spoke English.

So it was hard to learn to speak the language.

Yes, since I learned it from a schoolteacher who couldn't pronounce it. And when I learned it also from a professor who hated the French and had all the classes in English, it didn't help.

Why did you become interested in translating Quebecois and Acadian poets?

Why? Because, in a sense, that was supposed to be a part of my heritage. I'm not sure that it necessarily was because most of my ancestors were farmers. They didn't use any more words than they could help, in any language.

What do you think the role of the translator is?

The same as the role of the poet is. You are given an experience. You are given words and you try to put that experience and the new words that you use in such a way as to make what struck you in the first place clearer and, in a sense, more satisfactory to you than if you had just left it the way it was.

Do you feel frustrated by the act of translation? Some people think that it goes back to the idea of the translator being a traitor, traductore, being so close to traduttore. They think that you cannot translate from one language to another.

Yes, but you translate any time that you think. What you are doing is translating thought and action into words. You can do this as well in music, art, choreography, even the structures of games.

So you think we can translate the essential aspect from one language to another.

The essential. Exactly. You can put things into a language, even though it attempts to explain what happened thousands of years ago. In Seamus Heaney's translation of *Beowulf*, he uses many Irish words that are being used now; he discovered that these words were very old words that went way back, practically to the time of their origins. This adds a kind of bringing together of the human element. In a way it's like recognizing your grandfather.

So translation is part of our civilization, finding a connection to our civilization.

Exactly. That is, of course, the secret of religion in the holy books of any particular country, passed on through translation and has been so ever since language was discovered. When you study anthropology, for example, you will find linguistic anthropology. You are looking at a language of a primitive people. The language may include not only the people, but also the animal associated with what they have or it may include part of the environment that they exist in and they just don't add another word. They take it for granted that this word means all of these different things.

How close to the original do you try to get? There are two extremes of translation. On one extreme, the translator aims for a literal exactness, while at the other extreme, for example, Robert Lowell's Imitations, *the poet takes certain liberties with the text and almost writes a different poem.*

When I have gone to translation discussions, or whatever you call these things, there are two different schools that are still trying to compete with each other and the result is almost always inconclusive. I don't think that it matters too much what you do. What they all have in common is that they go beyond, that they find, in order to bring into being, something else that strikes them as being more satisfactory than what they had found when they first found it. Consequently, if theirs is more of a copying nature than anything else, they will go for the exact translation. On the other hand, if copying has less appeal to them than doing something of their own, then they are more likely to produce the kind of Robert Lowell translation that you are referring to. It is not always easy to know exactly where one begins and the other ends.

Like a spectrum.

And you use what you find in order to build on what you find.

What are the qualities of a good translator?

Well, for one thing, a good translator, if he finds the thing that at the heart of the poem is a living thought or a living situation or something that might be these things, will somehow or other emphasize these things in the particular work concerned. And it is most challenging if it is in a form like a sonnet of Hérédia's or somebody like that because Hérédia has used a chronological method that incorporates a thought per sitting. If you get a Hérédia sonnet and you turn it into an English translation, what you've got to do is do what it would take to write this particular type of sonnet. To accomplish this would be fine because that would add a new depth from you to the memory of the French that you saw in the first place. You would then have an English equivalent which would reinforce the French.

Then the new translation should be a poem in itself.

Yes, it should be a poem in itself. It is no harder to do than it is to write a poem by itself because the translation, the original poem, has given you a blueprint for a new poem.

How important are the structure and the line and other stylistic elements for you in translation?

It depends on the kind of poem that one is translating. If one is translating a poem, for example, that is told as a story and the story is important, don't get in the way of the story by cramming yourself; keep it spare and keep the good part until you come to the end. That will mean it may reverse everything or it may not, but whatever it does it focuses new light on what wasn't expected by what had come before that light had been shown.

For example, in the poems by Nelligan you use a similar kind of imagery, rhyme, sound and structure that he uses in order to stay close to the poetry.

The best poem by Nelligan, as far as I'm concerned, is "Tawny Landscape." The way I did it is better than any other of the poems I have put into English by Nelligan. Not that it is the best thing Nelligan has ever written in French, but as a translation into English, it probably is.

It is the best poem you have translated.

Which is interesting again. It's as good that way as much as Nelligan himself is good in that kind of way. It shows me a Nelligan that Edmund Wilson discovered as the first modern poet in North America to emphasize what modern poetry in the late nineteenth century saw as the basis of original poetry, the treatment of alienation between man and society. In poems like this one, leading to ultimate madness, Nelligan is a classic example.

How important is finding the right idiom for you?

Idiom can distill some things, sometimes, into a living expression. It wouldn't have been there if it just hadn't occurred to someone and very often it is a very slight kind of thing. I sometimes think many poems are written simply for the sake of their clever idiom.

I notice that in your writing you find equivalents for idioms in English and French which make for a strong translation.

It should be that way.

Douglas, New Brunswick, June 4, 2002

LOUIS DUDEK

It is a hot Montreal morning in late June. A breeze wafts through the trees as I drive from the Outremont plateau, along the tortuous Côtes des Neiges, down into the corridors of the city. The streets are quiet. Louis Dudek lives on a street nestled in Westmount, not far from the park and the library. It's from this corner that Dudek has carried on his work as a publisher, editor, professor, and poet. Dudek, Frank Davey observed, is the most influential of "any poet in Canadian literary history." He has been associated with *First Statement*, *Contact*, *CIV/n*, *Delta*, and D.C. Books. He has been committed to the development of literature throughout his life. This can be seen in his dissertation, *Literature and the Press*, his interest in Ezra Pound, and his desire to keep art independent of commercial influence.

It is a modest two-story red-brick house. Dudek appears relaxed this morning. He speaks about giving his last lecture, his last reading, and an upcoming book. One is immediately aware of an order in the house, a definite clarity of arrangement. Along the wall there is a twelve-foot bookcase. In fact, there are bookcases throughout the house, even in Dudek's legendary basement filled with magazines, periodicals and books. There are paintings by Louise Scott, influenced by Betty Sutherland, Irving Layton's second wife. "Aileen has arranged everything," Louis says. On a side table are several vases created by Wanda Rozynski, who was associated with *CIV/n*. There is Aileen's Henry Moore sketch, "Drawings of People in the Underground," from World War II. Dudek comments, "I'm not much in favour of it. I like people fully awake." There are two art books, Borduas and Miro. In the staircase there are paintings by Stella Sagatis, mother of Dudek's first wife. He says he has enjoyed living with these because they are filled with flowers and trees. In the dining room there is a reproduction of Da Vinci's "Madonna of the Rocks" and his unfinished picture of Saint Anne. Against the opposite wall is a Mac which Louis uses to write on and play chess against Sargon. A copy of *Open Letter* sits beside it. In the middle of the dining table is a bouquet of chrysanthemums. Louis says, "They cry out to be praised." We start the interview with Louis reading Sidney's translation of a Petrarch poem followed by his own version and inviting me to compare them.

In the poem "Life and Art" you wrote, "Life / first, and art after, if a choice / must be made." Is this an accurate statement of your aesthetics?

Yes. First, you notice that the phrasing contains

an aesthetic quality, or what I think of as the "electric charge." But why life first and art after? Because a choice must be made. That's the key. And of course it's simply true. It's made in a sharp epigrammatic way, but in fact I am affirming an order of values. My position has always been that art exists in order to serve life, to represent life, to discover some new possibility, a breakthrough for life itself. That's what it's all about. If we imagine something, we imagine something we might do, or could do, or could become.

Why were the 1950s in Montreal so crucial for the development of literature in Canada?

It's not something that happens to us; it's something that we do that makes a period important. In the 1950s we did that. When I came back in 1951, I came to teach at McGill. I came with the perfect confidence that I was coming where I had to be to do my important work. It was not just for myself that I was going to do this work, but for this city and this country. I was ready for it, and I knew it was going to be important. We were going to change our world, so to speak. Somehow that involved the many things I had learned in New York. I had studied modern poetry there. I had studied under Lionel Trilling, Jacques Barzun, and Emery Neff. I was full of the sense of what the modern is, and the transformation that modernism must bring to poetry and life. So I came back and a friendship was soon renewed with Irving Layton, and we began to publish together. The first book was *Cerebus* – three poets together, Layton, Dudek, and Souster, with prefaces by each.

At first it was just ourselves getting off the ground, but we were going to publish others. Daryl Hine was in Montreal at that time and his book soon appeared. Leonard Cohen turned up at McGill and he wanted to bring out a book, so actually I proposed that the McGill Poetry series start with his book. After that other books followed. At the same time Contact Press was bringing out books through Raymond Souster in Toronto and ourselves jointly in Montreal. And the first bunch of those I was editing from McGill.

Before us, a very important generation, the first modern generation, had done work from 1925 to 1940, but they had not started presses. They had published some magazines. These magazines, however, were not really little magazines in the real sense of young poets making very radical statements of their own. In the 1940s in *Preview*, *First Statement*, *Contemporary Verse* you got that for the first time. Since then, this kind of originality has spread all over Canada, a branch of independent writing and publishing. Because that other phase had preceded in the 1920s, the one in the 1940s looks so important. There was a lot of momentum behind it. The two generations joined together.

In the 1950s a number of poets were associated with

Frye: James Reaney, Jay Macpherson, D.G. Jones, and Eli Mandel. Mandel, in fact, called the fifties an "age of mythopoeia."

Sure, Mandel was one of the mythopoeic poets himself, so he would be inclined to call it that. It certainly wasn't mythopoeic in the 1950s. It contained the mythopoeic group appearing for the first time, as well as more general modernists who were still dominant. John Sutherland was one of the first admirers of James Reaney's book *The Red Heart* in 1949. I also thought Reaney was wonderful. I mean one was interested in any poet that really had that kind of jazz, that really had something alive, something exciting and different in him. You didn't want poets to be copies of one another. Of course, Raymond Souster was the ideal poet of our kind who was simple, straightforward and dealt with the contemporary world, people in the street. He had a humanitarian sympathy for everybody. Raymond Souster was representative that way, but at the same time he was, of course, limited in what he could do or say. One has to grow intellectually as well. Reaney was something different, formalist in his methods, and eccentric in his behaviour. Very bright.

Also, his mythological interests are connected to the earth and local history. The Donnellys *and other works have a strong sense of the local.*

That's true. That's probably often forgotten. In the mythopoeic group, whether in James Reaney or

Margaret Avison, there's a strong local realistic particularism that makes a firm bridge between them and the Montreal group. That realistic touch, that's the Canadian character. In films it becomes the documentary of the NFB, you see, utterly factual.

The local.

They were beginning there. In the fifties the mythopoeic group was beginning and important works by Northrop Frye were coming out. Then *Delta* came out in 1957. I published a review of Jay Macpherson which was very critical of her traditionalist mythopoeic kind of writing. However, she sent me some poems in response, and these too I published gladly. They were good things. So they were part of the mix and part of a lively debate. Controversy is good for poetry and for groups. There had been a controversy between *Preview* and *First Statement*, and now this controversy between the mythopoeic poets and the social realists. But then, who were the social realists? Is Irving Layton a social realist? My God, he's really some kind of a surrealist I would say, a rhetorical surrealist. Am I a social realist? Hardly at all. I'm more or less a transcendentalist in poetry. It's hard to say. Raymond Souster is the nearest to being a social realist, but even there, I would say this would be a very soft social realism.

Do you see a connection, then, between this social realist school and yourself, Irving Layton, Raymond Souster and the mythopoeic school? You have myth in your work in the same way the mythopoeic poets have an anchor in experience.

The point is that we were opposed to each other because of the exclusive concern with myth on the part of Frye and the actual rejection of the social realist position by Frye, with damaging remarks about it in the essay "Tarzanism in Canadian Poetry." "Tarzanism" he called it. He was often offensive, in his mild way, to the school of reality. There's a real temperamental opposition between the two, and one has to look at what's at the root of that. So I don't think that there's any congruence between the two things at all. The mythopoeic school was leading Canadian poetry in directions that were not helpful in the way that I thought we could develop in Canada.

I want to ask you about the change in the 1950s from a more formal literature, with its emphasis on the formal properties of literature, moving toward the poetry of voice, the poetry of experience as represented by Tish.

Yes, now that would have been in the 1960s that another kind of poetry came in, not mythopoeic and not social realist, but very much concerned with voice and sound. Reading aloud would never appeal to me nor the notion that some kind of new aesthetic would come out of this kind of plain sounding of poetry. I know all about the history of oral literature, of course. Homer and all that. But that was in an age of oral poetry, before the advent of writing.

If you know that, you must also know that literature was then written on a scroll, and that later still it became very strongly scripted, so that our experience of it was no longer pronounced with the lips, as the Romans still did, reading with their lips and reading aloud. We eventually learned not to have to do that at all because as human beings we had learned how to listen inside our heads. And the experience of reading that way became more analytical and more attentive to what's there on the page. It's not less aural. It's imagined. It's much more imaginative.

There's a strong sense of voice in your poems, a sense of colloquial speech, yet accompanying it is a structure, a philosophical argument. How did you develop the balance between these two aspects of your poetry?

I don't see any opposition. These two things are entirely compatible. You can have something that is extremely philosophical with an extremely formal and pompous tone of voice. You can have the philosophical with the colloquial, which brings it to life, which probably is what philosophical ideas need. They need somebody to make them come alive. *[Laughter.]* So you get this kind of voice. Primarily, the issue can be stated like this. I believe a poem ought to say something, because a poem that just babbles along and says nothing at all is just a pain in the ass. I don't like to hear somebody just sounding off out of vanity. I want meaning to be conveyed, at least some images that I can think about, if not some idea.

The short poem, "The Sea," for instance, is a very beautiful poem, rich in its qualities and voice. It foreshadows and contains many of the elements that are later expressed in your longer poems.

Yes. It's strange that you bring that up, because on Friday I'm visiting a class at McGill, and I've just agreed to talk to the students about this poem! And with the poem, I want to tell them just what you said, that this poem of the sea existed before I had ever seen the sea at all. It's full of the sense of a meaning that appears later in *Europe*. This whole idea of the sea is the unifying concept of that book. It's extraordinary that I hit upon an idea, a metaphor, which was going to do so much for my poetry later, not only in *Europe*, but also in *Atlantis* and other poems. So, of course, the Frye group would say that this is a deep image of the archetypal sort. Perhaps so, but it need not be that. There is W.H. Auden's book on the subject of the sea, *The Enchaffèd Flood*, the turbulent sea, all about the sea in literature, how much has been written about it. The whole question, then, is whether there's an archetypal image here or perhaps an experience so moving that it represents whatever ideas you may need, even as Niagara Falls does, or the starry sky, and you would be surprised if somebody thought there was nothing at all there, just a lot of water and empty space. You know, we're moved, we're so moved by the sea. I'm so overwhelmingly moved and propelled into thought by the sea that I have it all in the very first poem I wrote on seeing the sea: "Coming suddenly to the sea in my twenty-eighth year."

You have been critical of Frye's view of literature yet you use myths in your own writings, for example in Atlantis. *How is your use of myth different from Frye's?*

Now, the definition that I would want, if we're talking about myth philosophically, is something like "a story that has religious symbolism embedded in it, and is collective in its belief content," as in the Christian myth, or the Greek myths. If we limit it to that we'll be making sense of what we're saying because then other things that are not like that will be free of contamination. Words like "the sea" in my poetry are large metaphors; they are not really mythological. I say in *Europe*, "And I would not be surprised if the sea made Time / ... or if the whole fiction / of living were only a coil in her curvature." Now, how could the sea make time? It's an absurd statement. You could say that's absurd in a way that most mythological statements are absurd. The sea, the ocean could not make, create time. How could it create time? And yet when you read it in a poem and when I wrote it, it seemed perfectly valid poetically because metaphorically it is. But when I say "the sea" in the poem *Europe*, I am referring to something behind that word. It is that something that made time. And, "the whole fiction / of living were only a coil in her curvature…" of that creative process. So there is a creative reality of some sort as the source of all that exists. And you may say, if you are of a religious persuasion, "Oh, he obviously means God." Well, you can rush to your own conclusions if you wish. But I don't have any formulation about that, as yet. I am completely open on that question, and the point of this open-mindedness, which is very important to me, is to distinguish between what we know and what we do not know. What we know is what we know with our eyes, our ears, and our human relations, and through history so far as we know that. What we do not know is what we can suggest and intuit in poetry. It's very beautiful to know that we do not know it, that we can speak of it as the sea . . . or as "Atlantis", say, in another poem.

This is the source of your long poems.

That's right! You create another kind of metaphor. "Atlantis" is another large metaphor. The sea is the ocean which is visible. Atlantis is an imaginary continent that sank in the sea, and now it emerges bit by bit. It is used as a symbol for an ideal world, a utopia perhaps, an affection of some kind that surfaces out of the ocean, that surfaces out of reality. This is a metaphor of rich possibility, but it's not what it seems to be; it's only a metaphor for that something which also surfaced when Aileen brought a heap of chrysanthemums, white and red and pink, the beauty of those things sitting there on the table. They emerge out of somewhere, you see. That's where everything comes from, Atlantis. Here's a bit of Atlantis before us. *[Laughter.]*

It's interesting how you use the iceberg. Writers feel differently about icebergs. Roberts' iceberg is very different from Pratt's or from Purdy's iceberg.

You're right, Laurence, because it is the thought that surrounds the idea of an iceberg that will make it feel different for different people. For me it's the idea of Atlantis, and the iceberg is somehow related to that infinite source of visions, perfections, utopias ... and death also, with its coldness. So that it has a richness of feeling in it that makes it seem different. And it's at the end of *Atlantis* that the iceberg appears. So I would say that there are, in my poems of the sea, a whole cluster of metaphors. "Europe," itself, is a symbolic word and place. Interpreted, you could probably say it means something like "the civilized life." It means cities and nations with cathedrals, museums, books, and cultures, with all those possibilities of civilized life. Europe. I go to the heart of it, to the Parthenon from which everything in Europe derives. Europe, the sea, Atlantis. Is the sea Europe? Yes and no. *En México* is the jungle which is also an aspect of the sea, an aspect of the creative process, but here it's the negative aspect. The point of the jungle is that there everything is crowding everything out. The birds are shrieking, murdered. Everything is dying, choking inside that jungle. I've written an epigram, "In nature all forms of life are stunted."

Generally critics have not observed the importance of formal patterns in your work. There are exceptions, of course, such as Dorothy Livesay and Frank Davey. These formal patterns are important in the longer poems Europe, En México, *and* Atlantis. *Could you comment on formal elements such as line arrangement, rhythm and sound pattern.*

For a poet writing, these are the chief concerns. I don't think about the idea of the poem very much when I'm working on a poem, or I don't think about anything but the words of which it is made, how it flows together and how it is architecturally shaped. That is the poem. Because ultimately... suppose I've got a poem and it's a pretty good poem, but mediocre... the last line has a very bad word there and it just flops; it's lousy, the poem's no good. It's no good unless I'm terribly lucky and I find a replacement for that word in the last line that'll just lift it suddenly and make it a better poem. So you see, it's just that one word and you could prove it by taking any line of Shakespeare and changing it. You know, "the multitudinous seas incarnadine."

I was just thinking of that word.

Change "multitudinous" into something like "incarnadine multiplicity" and you know there's something wrong with that word "multiplicity." Unless you find the right word, you haven't got a poem. Everyone knows that. Finally the words are what the poem is made of and the words are, in a sense, magical. They are fitted like pieces in a jigsaw just exactly to fit into that position. That's it. Click! It works. But that perfection is actually in the words. Now, let's see if we answered the question about the importance of formal elements, such as line arrangement. Very important. Line arrangement. You see, I think that literature, poetry or the human mind itself have always had a very dangerous failing, a tendency to slip into the rut of mathematical counting, of lines, syllables, lengths, and thinking it has got a form when it has measured it out with a ruler or counting device, ten syllables to the line. So you have the heroic couplet. You have the French couplet and so on. This is really a perversion of artistic form, since the mathematics should be invisible, like that of flowing water or clouds. The twentieth century discovery is that form in the arts is more like modern dance, that it has an infinite number of forms that are made by free movement actually, with language and words. The only way to do it is the intuitive way, which is through feeling or aesthetic awareness.

Some of your poems are almost like the forms of paintings or ideograms, the way you see them on the page.

Absolutely. The beauty of an arrangement on the page that hits the eye, I love that. I want to read the poem when I see that it's a lovely scattering of a certain kind. I can see that it is done sensitively like a Japanese awareness of space. One of the articles by a Japanese student in *Delta* magazine was about the importance of space.

The Mac allows me a wonderful sense of kinesthesia of the poem.

The Macintosh helps, but of course the typewriter did it too, so this technique has a history. The line arrangement means that you don't indent all lines to the margin on the left hand side. You don't have a straight margin entirely. You indent in different ways and there are various points of indentation. And then not too much of that either, so that it doesn't look like a Ferlinghetti scattering; it's not salt and pepper. Actually there is a pacing. The way lines move in and back to the margin is a kind of lovely movement, more or less graceful, the way tropical fish move in the tank. It should be delightful and it should be well-paced.

It's also art, dance and music . . .

Yes, beautiful. Art, dance, music, in the way the words are moving around from the margin into the middle and so on. That's it. So therefore, line arrangement.

Critics often ignore these important aspects, even silence or the space between words.

Yes, but you see, for a critic to write about this is very difficult. He may perceive it and feel it, but then what's he going to say about it when he can't reduce it to mathematics? The only thing he can say is, "Isn't that fine the way this line drops here?" Now, in *Atlantis,* very often I found I'd have a line of about five or six words, then a break, with a highly indented part of a line with about four words, and then back to the margin with two or three or four words. This kind of three-line stanza must have some relation to the terza rima.

Exactly, I was just thinking it's Dante.

Inevitably, but it's so irregular that you could say it's got nothing to do with terza rima. There's no rima in there and there's no definite metric. But there's a threeness there. A kind of ta ta ta – ta ta – ta ta ta. This three-line shape has form; three is an interesting number, you know. Three-leaf clover. Nature must have discovered it and used it quite a lot. A rhythm. I guess a repetition is necessary. You could scan some of these things, but rhythm and metre are two different things. A rhythm and a metre. Sound pattern is the most beautiful way, yes.

You said in a recent interview that you consider Continuation *your best work.*

I suppose I do because it is the most completely worked out, a case of finding a voice for myself in the poetry. I explain that in the interview with Louise Schrier in *Zymergy 8*. In *Continuation 1* and *Continuation 2*, I at last found a voice where I could say exactly what I want to say, and everything I want to say, in the most amazing fragmentary way.

And you don't find the absence of a larger structure restricting?

Now what you want to say is, "Don't you mean it

has a flaw in it?" Yes, maybe it has. Even I may be aware of that, but you have to take risks in poetry. What is poetry trying to do on the page? It's trying to represent the poet's thought. If that's what it's trying to do, then ultimately you have to create a fictitious form that is doing that. Not one that is spurious, but the actual thought with all its fragmentary wayward digressions. And yet, if you read *Continuation 1* and *2*, you find that it's really not digressing so very much. It's actually obsessively concerned with only one kind of subject.

Essentially, the poem is concerned with process, getting closer to process.

The process is the internal monologue, only that part of it in the mind which deals with this question, which is poetry. But it's as if you were listening to me thinking as if it were recorded.

It's an important "as if."

As if. And I think eventually anybody can read that and say that it's easy as pie. They'd say, I've learned how to read him because I know what he really is deeply concerned with. That's what he's thinking about all the time and it's very amusing.

But still some of those individual lines are very well crafted. They have a subtle sense of sound, image and metaphor.

Sure, Laurence. Individual lines are well crafted. You may still have the feeling that somehow one line and the next one are not connected enough. That is a criticism that I've heard here and there. Maybe people have to get rid of the expectation that there's going to be a Wordsworthian boring exposition going on for six hundred lines on the same subject, that this talking old sheep is going to go on and on. This is not what this poem is doing. This poem is going to be exciting, or surprising, from line to line. But then, you no longer expect a connected essayish kind of mind here, or an old bore to be talking like Wordsworth. Then you may say, "This is very much like what happens in my own head."

So you should revise expectations...

Yes, expectations, but you also know that this is true, that this is true to nature, that this is true to your own thoughts. As you are sitting there your thoughts are jumping around. And since that is what is happening, that's what we want from literature. We want to know how human thought jumps about. And I guess it jumps about a little differently in every head and in every age. As time goes on, this poem is going to be dated and then they will say: "So that's how they thought in 1989... or the 1960s or 1970s."

What are the problems facing the English Quebec poet?

I would say there are none. The poet will be writing poetry whether there's a revolution or a war going on or not – as when Goethe during a war was quietly writing his poetry. During World War II German poets were writing when the bombs were falling and the concentration camps nearby were steaming full blast. The poet goes on writing for some reason. You might curse him for this, but that's the way it is. He does his work. The one thing to understand about the big events, the wars and revolutions, is that while the revolution is in progress, the people are still going to see plays, they're going to buy their lunch, and they're sitting and talking in cafés. Life is still going on even in the worst of times. That's so, always. The English-speaking population of Montreal is declining, and of course that affects the English Quebec poet, but they were never a great reading audience anyway. Our readers are scattered throughout Canada. We could be only ten people writing poetry in Quebec and no other English people here and we could still be known to some readers across Canada. That would still be possible. So as poets, we have no problems, really; you write your poetry. And for your lifetime, it will probably continue to be that way. On the other hand, there are immense problems of a practical sort. I am extremely critical of nationalism, which is a mode of transferred religious fanaticism. You know, that's what it really is, a group identity manifesting itself with a religious enthusiasm. Nationalism compensates for a sense of inadequacy or inferiority, and it ought to be dealt with at that level; we ought to do something about ourselves, do something positive rather than get up collectively and start yelling about how great we are, what giants we are. Today's *Gazette* deals with that, how the French see themselves as giants in Quebec. They aren't, of course, because they don't feel that they're giants. They're compensating. Well, I'm not a prophet and I don't want to be one. I hope these problems that we have in Quebec can be resolved. It's the only way we can prosper together, the French and the English both. I am certain that if we break up we'll be poorer and sadder and less productive in every way.

Do you see much interchange between French and English writers in Quebec and also in other parts of Canada?

Take a group like Guernica. Antonio D'Alfonso does have contacts with French writers. He is doing something. I know Claude Péloquin. He's a very good poet, very well known, and there's a translation of one of his books brought out by Guernica for which I wrote a preface. But that's a very rare exception. We have very little interchange between French and English writers. A few months ago *Liberté* asked for a response from English writers about the Quebec problems. I contributed to that; others did. The most memorable ones came from Henry Beissel and myself. We said what we really thought of this question. And they published a whole number of English responses to the French problem. Interchange there is little enough, but there would be enough if we read the French writers in their own texts and that's something that every English writer should do. I would say this to every writer in Canada. Read the other poets. Don't read only your own work and write your own poetry. Read and study the other poets so that you understand what each poet is saying in his own particular way. Read the Quebec poets too, and consistently study them, to find out what it is that each poet is saying, each as a separate voice. Don't be too quick to generalize about French writers.

Apropos of this in Zymergy 6, *David Solway says, "And I think as English poets we have an immense amount to learn from French poets in this country and they are on the whole the better poets."*

It's an impression one will get certainly from time to time, if you read French poetry and you talk to them, but it's much more complex than that. The French tend to be quite uppity, I would say, and that's one of their problems. Their intellectual life is very arrogant, and therefore cut off from their own people. A magazine like *Liberté* has no hopes of being read by very large numbers of French people. It's only for intellectuals and the university crowd that it's written. Its tone is quite wrong, I would say, as a literary magazine. They don't have any magazine of the kinds that we have had in English, like *Matrix, Delta*, or *Northern Review*, that is, magazines for the general reader that have relevant things to say about the whole culture and are open in a general way.

There have been exchanges between Quebecois femi-

nist poets Brossard, Cotnoir, Bersianik, Mouré, and Marlatt.

You see that's true, and there was an exchange between Frank Scott and Anne Hébert, though I don't know all the contexts that exist. There are the human interchanges between individuals and there are the books. I think it is more important that we read the books. There are two literatures here, not one, two language literatures. You cannot merge them into one, but you can build relations, and it's very enriching to do that.

What is the relevance of critical theory to poets?

Well, by critical theory you mean structuralism, post-structuralism, deconstruction, all that. I hope it's a passing fashion; it's junk, it's horrible, and its effect on literature and especially on the study of literature in universities has been totally negative. Critical theory, apart from that, as thinking about the nature of art, is very important. So that has to be distinguished. Current "critical theory" is a specific kind of fundamental, metaphysical approach, mainly denoted by the word "deconstruction." It is a linguistic metaphysics, which asks, "What is language? What are words and communications? What do we mean when we say, 'This is a fan'?" And finding that we don't know, or we don't mean anything, and that all languages are essentially ambiguous or meaningless, that nothing exists, is the same old philosophical nonsense about whether this table exists. "We can't prove that anything is so because of the nature of language." It's that sort of thing.

Is that what they're saying?

Of course. They're throwing great doubt on the nature of the literary act and communication itself. Certainly they are. The plain synonym for deconstruction is destruction.

But aren't they suggesting the many ways in which one can approach a text?

We always knew we could approach a text in many ways. What you really have is an approach that makes it impossible for most students to take literature now at the university. They don't want to study this subject. It's not literature anymore; it's become something else. It's something called "a philosophical theory about the nature of literature and language." They should set up a department called the philosophy of language and leave literature alone for those who want to study literature. As most poets and novelists will tell you, literature deals with telling a story or writing a poem. The thought about what that means is secondary and also many-sided. You can say many things about the same story or the same poem. Your response, of course, is very important; the kind of imagination and emotion you bring to it and the thoughts that you produce as to what you think it means. All that matters, of course, and it's a whole variety of things. But critical theory, as the French have developed it, is a kind of *a priori* methodology or metaphysics, and it's also a language. It's an incredible jargon which is only putting off the general reader. That's what its purpose is. And it should be very simple to see that a language is one that either wants to include people or one that wants to exclude people.

At McGill you encouraged young poets. It was a very healthy situation.

I myself am not typical of anything, since I was a maverick, and I did a few things out of my own convictions. But today's universities, how far have I looked into this? It's just a few casual contacts and the people I know who tell me what's happening at universities. Yes, the universities have been invaded by this critical methodology. They also have been invaded by Marxism in a very widespread way. It's all hush-hush about this; you don't want to stir up a new wave of McCarthyism. But Marxism, it seems, has taken over the universities; it has infiltrated everywhere. And what do we think Marxism is, a fine theoretical way of thinking? It's a program for *revolution*, don't you know? And here it is, all over the political science department, sociology, literature. It's everywhere, and behind critical theory, too, there are Parisian Marxists whose purpose is to overthrow the entire, so to speak, liberal humanistic civilization of the West, the death of the author being one of their latest findings. At first an idea, but then obviously later on it will be a reality when they put us up against the wall and shoot us. The death of the author is a figure of speech, but it can become quite a reality. They don't want the individualist author to be an important personage any longer. Individualism must go. They want just the text, and they want you to treat it in such a way that literature cannot be used as a support for individualism, or free thought.

What are you working on now? In "The Idea of Art" you speak about poets developing new forms of poetry. What are some of these possibilities?

The new forms of poetry are infinite, I believe. They do have affinities with preceding poetry because everything grows out of something else, but they also branch out in an incredible way, almost the way that plant life develops into a multitude of plant forms and leaf forms and so on. It is in this way that poetic forms can develop. They don't have to be mathematically structured, as we said earlier, but once they are released from that, there's no end of possibilities. You want to guard against two things, against a mathematical and geometrical structure, because it's too rigid. It freezes the process. The other is to watch that it does not become prose, that it does not go into the prose paragraph. The rhythm or the patterning – whatever it is – that movement or feeling with which you started determines that this is a poem. And once given, that you have that, that you're writing a poem, you can make many poems.

It's very much up to the individual poet. The young

poet has a map of what he wants to do, like Wordsworth, or Rimbaud in "The Poet at Seven." He is constantly looking for new forms as you did in the early work and later in Continuation I *and* 2.

That's my development of the form; it evolves like a plant. But, take certain experimental forms that I developed. If you go back to the seventeenth century, the emblem poems in which a poem imitates the shape of something, well, that was the first of its kind. Then, the next important step, I would say, is Mallarmé and the poem *Un coup de dés*, "A throw of the dice," where the words are scattered, because he's trying to say something about chance. *Un coup de dés n'abolit pas le hazard* (A throw of the dice does not abolish chance). Of course, rather a self-evident statement. Anyhow, that's a wonderful poem of Mallarmé's that had a powerful effect upon me. The emblem poems, and Mallarmé, show that you can take words out of the rigid form of the coffin-like quatrain. You can really scatter the words and you can do something strikingly new, like the extreme innovations of Walt Whitman, or Apollinaire, or cummings. Whitman was aware that he had released the poem from the quatrain by making this long line of his of various lengths and letting it speak – a wonderful release. But he also had the emotion that made sure it never lapses into mere prose. He's compelled by an almost transcendental quality of feeling. That's it. Now, starting from that, and looking at what other poets have since done, depending on your individual temperament, there's no end of forms that can emerge and one would want to live forever to see what poets will write. That's where the infinite worlds are, in part.

Each decade you can develop different forms, do variations on them.

Variations, yes. Let's think about that. In music, you make a melody, then you compose variations. That's very important for structure in music, because in music they develop the structure of sound by making variations on a theme. You think of "The Goldberg Variations" or the "Chaconne." So in poetry perhaps we haven't thought much of variations, but if you look at *Continuation 1* and *2* you may say, "What he's got here are variations." As Mike Gnarowski said, "You know, you're saying the same thing over and over." I never repeat myself entirely, but actually if you examine it, and you number these things or see them in different colours, you might get a sense of variation in the way it occurs. It's the way the ideas turn and return. There's the possibility here that variation may have a future in poetry. Remember that Eliot worked the *Four Quartets* on the theory of imitating musical form. Ezra Pound said there was a fugal form in *The Cantos*, an idea which I don't think he carried very far, but he had it in his mind in the early cantos. Ezra Pound is important here because of the form, let's say, in *The Pisan Canto* – very highly charged poetically and very free in the way the lines move. That's the nearest to the kind of thing I eventually did. But I have never really followed Ezra Pound. I found my own form in my own way.

Montreal, Quebec, June 25, 1992

AL PURDY

Driving south of Belleville I take Highway 62 over the arched bridge that leads from Hastings to Prince Edward County. It's August 8, 1991, and I'm on my way to interview Al Purdy. One of the most influential Canadian poets during the last three decades, he has published forty books: poetry, anthologies, essays, letters, and a novel. I remember first meeting him at the launch of *Storm Warning 2*, the poetry anthology he brought out with McClelland & Stewart in 1976, which included two of my poems. I haven't seen Purdy since the early 1980s at the International Authors Festival at Hart House where he read poems from *The Stone Bird*.

I see this landscape of Prince Edward County through Purdy's poems. At a corner where the forest is beginning to encroach on the field, a farmer on his tractor makes a turn, and I think of the farmer from "The Country North of Belleville," "plowing and plowing a ten-acre field until / the convolutions run parallel with his own brain – " When I enter Ameliasburgh, I cannot help but think of *In Search of Owen Roblin.* I turn, following Purdy's instructions, pass a library that was established in 1842, and then turn into the lane where Purdy lives. A few houses down I see a Ford parked in the driveway, and know this must be the place. As I get out of my car, I see the tall familiar figure with his long angular strides approaching me. "You must be staying close to here. You're right on time."

Inside, Al Purdy talks about this house on Roblin Lake that he and his wife, Eurithe, built. They began in 1957, adding the part where we are standing in 1974-1975. "It was continually being built for a long time. I don't know when you would say it was finished." He invites me outside and points to the spire across the lake telling me that it is the church from "Wilderness Gothic." "It is now a museum." He speaks of earlier days when there weren't as many houses on Roblin Lake, "I had to cut a hole in the ice which was a hell of a job. The ice gets to be over three feet thick." Purdy says that he has seen cranes on the shore in the morning. As we speak, an otter surfaces near the shore. Roblin Lake has become much noisier, and he is trying to have motor boats banned.

Purdy leads the way along a wooden walkway to his study. "My wife doesn't come in here because she thinks it disturbs me." On the walls behind his desk are copies of poems, photographs of writers, and a large poster of his old friend, Earl Birney. On the bookshelves, which extend nearly to the ceiling, are exclusive editions of *On the Bearpaw Sea* and *The Quest For Ouzo*. He shows me a Governor General's Award copy of *The Collected Poems of Al Purdy* with an ivory seal on the cover. "Awful colours blue and green together," he says. Recently he has been to Charlottetown to accept the Milton Acorn Award for his collection *The Woman on the Shore*. At present he is working on the final chapter, "Anecdotage," of his autobiography "Reaching for the Beaufort Sea."

We continue the interview in the living room with Al Purdy across from me facing a window. Two pictures on his wall, one of a young half-naked girl, another of a man wearing a sombrero, are reminiscent of D.H. Lawrence's watercolours. The bookcases are nearly empty now; Purdy's library has been bought by Avie Bennett, who donated it to the University of Toronto. Al is alone this morning. Eurithe has gone back out to Sidney on Vancouver Island, where they are renovating their house.

In your prefaces and other writings you are continually speaking of "influence." Why is this question of influence important for you?

Because mostly it seems important to other people. Other people are always talking about influences. Well, as a matter of fact, I think it is interesting too. Don't you ever wonder how you happen to be writing the way you are and who influenced you and whether you submerged those influences or not? My own go a long way back. I suppose the last one was probably D.H. Lawrence. The other writers that I admire, such as W.B. Yeats or W.H. Auden, I can't learn anything from. They are just too much themselves.

Writing is also concerned with the making of yourself.

What do you mean?

Once you absorb writing, you change in some way.

You take the work someone else is writing. If it's been important to you, you change somewhat. The ideal is to absorb other people's writing and influences and from the outside nobody is able to know that. You don't want to look as if you're imitating someone else. If you are yourself, you have added yourself to all of those other influences.

Do you have any predominant impressions of the years you spent out West during the war?

They're all through the poems. You can rehash them now, but your memory is the memory of the poems, really. Well, just a minute. I should say I have one memory that I don't think is in the poems, that time from just after I had gotten married. Both my wife and myself were in Vancouver at the time, when I got word that I was transferred to Woodcock, about eight or nine hundred miles up in the far northern interior of British Columbia. And there I was wifeless, in the wilderness. I wrote to a flight sergeant I knew back in Vancouver in the orderly room, "I want to get transferred back." Christ, I'm just married and all this crap. At the same time as I tried to get transferred, I also tried to get my wife a travel warrant which meant she could travel for nothing. Suddenly, unbeknownst to me, the travel warrant came through for her. So my wife started to come up to Woodcock. But also I got transferred back to Vancouver. We passed each other about half way. When Eurithe got to Woodcock she got a job in the airmen's mess, waiting on tables or whatever it was. She liked it up there; it was right in the wilderness, and she wouldn't come back. And there I was, wifeless, back in Vancouver, going nuts, getting jealous as hell.

In the mid-1950s you went to Montreal where you met Milton Acorn.

Yes, I stopped in Montreal on the way to Europe in 1955, and stayed with Layton, slept on his studio couch as I recall. And when I came back in 1956, I decided I wanted to go to Montreal. Yes, I met Milton Acorn. I believe that Layton sent him over because I had a couple of plays on the CBC and Milton wanted to get some hints on playwriting. We yakked away for a long time.

Acorn was not only a writer, but a friend; you had a lot of things in common: your socialism, nationalism, playwriting.

Yes, he was quite an influence. I realized to my shock after quite a while, that he was writing much better than I was. That was too hurtful at the time to admit. When I first knew him he was terrible. He had published a chapbook; it was just awful, too many clichés. At the same time he was writing new poems that were terrific. It was his best stuff really. He had many periods of writing in which he changed a great deal. He became very diffusive later on. Right at the time I knew him he was writing at his best for six or seven years. I have a theory that you have a period of five to ten years in which you are at your best, and that after that you deteriorate. I admire Layton. I don't think he's writing very well right now, but the way he was writing a few years ago he was the best in Canada. I mean that's what you ought to judge a poet by, his best or her best. I prefer to judge, say, Margaret Avison by her best, which was also a few years ago.

Which decade was that for you?

Well, I don't know. It's up to other people to make that ... Jesus, look at the chipmunk up on top of that, see on top of that little peak there. *[Chuckles.]* I think he's got a home in there. That's the pump house. There's a well right underneath that.

Around the late 1950s you moved from Montreal to Ameliasburgh.

Oh yes. I was exceedingly broke at the time and it was very expensive to live in Montreal. We wanted to build a house. I had been writing plays in Montreal and I sold two or three of them. I had ten or twelve hundred dollars. A government building was being torn down in Belleville, so I think I paid five hundred dollars for the stuff. We built the house ourselves. That may be obvious. Probably none of the corners is square; that is in a lot of poems too. My wife and I went broke here, so we had to go back to Montreal to get jobs again and leave the house to its own devices. The second time we came back, well, my mother was growing very old. We had a bit more money and I had gotten a thousand dollars from the Canada Council to go out West. I came back with Milton Acorn in the very late spring. This was the time when he was helping me with the other part of the house. In my opinion his abilities as a carpenter grew very much less as I watched him work. Well, he put all the cross pieces in as if we had never levelled them right, so I had to do that all later. However, I'm not denigrating Acorn in any way. He was quite a man. I wish he had taken more baths though. He is just getting a little more attention now that he's dead than he ever did when he was alive. This business of the award in his name is a good thing because at his best I think he was a marvellous poet; at his worst he was so bad. He was one of those poets from whom you can both learn what to do and what not to do at the same time.

You wrote a number of plays in the 1950s. Did the writing of these plays have an effect on your own poetry?

Letter writing probably had an effect on my ability to write because I wrote so many letters. I must have had twelve or fifteen plays produced for CBC.

They were mostly radio plays. One was on television, which was later put on stage in Toronto called *Just Ask for Sammy*. Yes, it had a hell of an influence on me. You get a facility with words through sheer practice in writing and working at it.

Most of your poems have a dramatic element in them.

Glad to hear it.

Dennis Lee wrote in his afterword to the Collected Poems, *that there was an abrupt quantum leap in your poetry around 1960-1962.*

Oh, sure. You change as you grow older. Your mind changes and you get more complicated and realize things are not so simple as you thought them. Yes, around 1962 with *Poems for All the Annettes* I consciously changed. I realized how bad my stuff had been, which is something that not too many people do about their own work. *[Laughter.]*

Was there any other period, after the 1970s, when you went through a change like that?

Well, I think there have been several changes. The result of that change with *Poems for All the Annettes* was *The Cariboo Horses*. Then there was a period after the time of *Wild Grape Wine* from 1970-1975. I was in the doldrums. It took a long time before I realized that I was not writing well. After about 1977-1978 I started to change again. The drama diffused through the poem. I mean I wrote poems in which other people, much more than myself, were the interesting element. Of course, your comments on them are you anyway.

So there is another change around the end of the 1970s.

Let's say 1979 to the present time. I have always being accused of being elegiac, and I guess I am. But it seems to me that elegiac quality is an area in which you can write very well because we mourn the past continually, I think. Back there we were too stupid to mourn it. We were living it. And we don't appreciate the past. And now is the past, actually. It is rapidly becoming the past.

This morning is already the past. It has become history. The great poets W.B. Yeats, T.S. Eliot and Rilke have this elegiac quality.

I can't appreciate Rilke. There are an awful lot of poets for whom I have a dead ear. I appreciate Yeats a great deal. I appreciate Thomas, and a lot of others, but I can't appreciate Rilke. It may be the translation. A guy named Leishman translated him. And he used metre and rhyme. I don't see anything to it.

The translator makes the poem. Sometimes it's the translation that we respond to.

In that connection I've got a book called *Poets on Street Corners* which is a bunch of translations of Russian poems. There are translations of Anna Akhmatova by several people. One translation of "Requiem" is by Robert Lowell. And I thought it was terrific, but he has been accused of irregularities in translating that. I don't care if he has been or not, he made it a poem. That is a terrific poem. I don't particularly like Lowell's own poems, but his translations, some of them are just marvellous.

Around the 1980s or earlier you started to read South Americans, in particular, Neruda. One of your poems ends "of my residence on earth," which comes from the title of a Neruda book.

I read some of the translations of Neruda which I thought were extraordinary. There are other South American poets as well, Vallejo. But I haven't been reading them very much lately. You have periods in which you do this, read translations.

Did reading Neruda change your perspective?

No, not really. I mean it made me realize that there was a lot of good stuff. Robert Bly came out with a magazine called *The Sixties*, and then later, *The Seventies*, in which there were many translations, and I read James Dickey. My own influences are almost all British. And yet I don't like British poems these days at all.

When you say nearly all British, would you clarify that?

I loved A.E. Housman for instance, but I don't write particularly like Housman at all. The American I like best is probably Jeffers as much as anyone, Robinson Jeffers.

What is it you see in Jeffers?

I think that when you ride a hobbyhorse the way Jeffers and Housman have, then it becomes a mannerism. Do you really feel and think the way you're writing at all times? I don't know. The same thing has gone on with Bukowski. He writes the same way all the time. His subjects are hardly ever varied. What do I see in Jeffers? I see an attitude, a way of thinking that is at variance with most people's way of thinking. It is pleasant to see someone who doesn't agree with everybody else. You don't want to read someone who agrees with everybody else. Of course, you're supposed to be upbeat in the world and be optimistic about everything: "God's in his heaven / All's right with the world!" And I like Browning. I like an awful lot of British poets, but not the current ones. The only other current one that I like a bit is Ted Hughes. But what I like of Hughes is in the past too, his first two or three books. I don't like his last ones all that much. The great difficulty in anybody's writing is that you agree with somebody else's opinions. You read the anthology choices. The big ones are saying, "I'm talking about the ones I like." Well, I don't want anybody to agree with me in what I like. I just like people to look at all the stuff themselves and see what they think because the tendency is to be influenced. I don't want to be influenced beyond a certain point. You've got to be influenced, up to a point.

There's also a part of you that is yourself and won't be influenced anyway because it's you.

I'm annoyed by people trying, trying to influence me. There is a quality about all the big anthologies that say this is the canon, this is the good stuff.

Do you have a feeling of this today, that there is a particular canon that is privileged?

Well, for a long time the *Tish* boys were a particular west coast gang that had its influence, as the Black Mountain did.

Has writing criticism helped you to define things you wouldn't have been able to otherwise?

I suppose so. Some people tend to go along with the general opinion of somebody else. I hope that I can look at it objectively, to some extent, to see what I think of it, rather than agreeing with everybody else, or simply disagreeing for the sake of disagreeing. Nowlan's early stuff was quite wonderful, but in his last few years he stayed home and wrote poems about things that he read rather than experienced. Of course, we all do that out of the past. I got two or three poems out of E.M. Forster's essays, one about Voltaire, for instance. I like Forster very much, his essays particularly, much more so than his fiction.

Some of your poems such as "Transient" and "Elegy for a Grandfather," have been published in several versions.

Particularly "Elegy for a Grandfather." I have never been satisfied with the ending of that. I am still not quite satisfied. I have probably revised it in the last few months. Yes, I have gone through several versions. I don't think that just because you publish a poem that it means it's immune. You generally have to copy your old poems sooner or later anyway, you know, type them again or whatever. When you do so you may grow dissatisfied with this or that. And if you're dissatisfied with something you want to change it, don't you?

In "Transient" you took the passage about the Indian girl and changed that three or four times.

Oh yes, I did change that, I remember that well. It was rather stilted I thought and sounded like somebody else, the Indian whore up on a balcony, who could quite possibly have been a Coast Salish princess anyway, but I think this is fantasy.

Do you keep a poem in your head a long time before you actually put it down?

I am sure you know that if you want to write a poem or if you've got some lines in your head, you'd better write it right away or you forget it. The inclination goes completely if you don't write it. There have been denials of that, for instance, this poem "Grosse Isle." I read about the cholera epidemic in Quebec and the rest of Canada when I was reading up for purposes of the novel, so I knew a fair amount about cholera beforehand. Then I saw this article in the *Globe and Mail*, which was long and informative, and I thought my God that's almost a poem in itself.

So I scribbled up the page of the *Globe and Mail*, lines for the future poem. Then I flew out to the West Coast with my wife for the winter where we have a house, and I forgot about that poem for two or three months. And then I came across it, and I thought well I better write the damn thing or I will never write it, and it came back. Then I thought that the Auden line, "Look, stranger, on this island now," would fit for an epigraph because Auden's island was a pleasant island, "The leaping light for your delight discovers." That's a pleasant island. This is not a pleasant island, Grosse Isle. It's such an opposite that it fits as an epigraph. So I wrote the poem. And that's about all there is to it.

With the publication of The Stone Bird *your style changed again.*

Yes, it did.

There is a refinement of tone, a strong sense of wonder at the physical world.

There was less of myself as a dramatic happening, in any sense, in it. It is other people who have taken over the poem, very largely I think from that point on. When you read "Grosse Isle," which is the last poem that I have, that I think is a decent poem. I am not in that poem very much except as a matter of opinion. Yes, I am just not there.

In some of your other strong poems, such as "Wilderness Gothic," "Menelaus and Helen," and "The Runners," you are also absent.

Well, they are earlier poems, except for "Menelaus and Helen," which is a later poem. But then the sense of drama is so strong that it has taken over completely. The point that you have got to remember in all these things is that somebody is writing these, so that he or she is always there from that point.

Yet you are still writing poems which have that personal drama, "Lost in the Badlands," for example.

Ah ha, in which I was very much present. *[Much laughter.]* Well, again these things do happen. And they do suggest poems. My wife has been a very strong source of writing poems or subjects for poetry all of my life, or all the last forty years or so.

Speaking of your wife, in your work sometimes the woman is more perceptive, as in "The Tarahumara Women," or she changes the perception of the male speaker, as in "The Horseman of Agawa."

Oh, sure. My wife is a very perceptive woman, but she is not nearly so verbal. And I'm completely verbal. My thought and my words flow equally at the same time; they are absolutely synchronous.

The woman, then, is a source of inspiration for these poems.

I don't know if she is a source of inspiration. I don't like the word "inspiration." I hate the word. But there is a male-female thing, between a man and a woman that occasionally produces drama or something interesting which I am using, of course. I am also thinking of "Over the Hills in the Rain, My Dear." The last lines are, "but to be a fool / is sometimes / my own good luck."

In Woman on the Shore *you wrote about the importance of Margaret Laurence.*

I respected her a great deal. She was a very much respected woman. She was also a fine writer. In a way I am almost sorry that she came back to Canada. Her drive had to do with being isolated in England, being alone with the kids; of course the kids grew up. She had a lot of friends in Canada, but I think when she came to Canada, she did not write any more novels because she was reaping the rewards of being a writer. From that point of view, it was probably bad for her, as a writer, to come back to Canada. She would probably have written another novel or two. I corresponded with her for a very long time.

You stayed with her for a while when you were in England.

My wife had an operation in 1969. She was very kind to us, particularly then, and we used to get into discussions or arguments. Basically underneath all the iconoclasm, she was a religious woman, whereas all my religion is anti-religious. But she wouldn't admit that on the surface very much, I don't think. Well, she would I suppose. It's hard to say.

What about the references in your poem, "The Darkness," to "religion / not the conventional stuff."

Well the religious sense, but it's certainly not any conventional religion. And it is not even provable. Nothing is provable anyway, if it comes to that. I mean however fervent our gospel singers around are, they can't prove a damned thing. I mean they can't prove it the way two and two are four. You can never see any God, no matter how much you think you can.

What about the references to the Bible in your poems?

Well, what about them? Religion is bound to be a part of your life, even if you don't believe in a God. I mean probably the only tenable position is agnosticism anyway which says, "Show me."

D.H. Lawrence becomes an important subject for you. In a recent poem published in Quarry *you talk about Lawrence, Christ, and Roblin's Mills. Could you talk about this poem and your interest in Lawrence?*

Well, the thing about Lawrence, and one of D.H. Lawrence's admittedly large influences was Walt Whitman. I don't like the sound of Whitman. I don't like Whitman at all, anybody who walks down the road slapping everybody on the back and saying, "Hail fellow . . ." All this shit would bore the hell out of me. I am who I am and I like who I like as the case may be, and of course, Lawrence, whether he admitted it or not, was that same way too. He didn't like everybody he met. He was a very prickly character. I doubt, if I met him personally, I would have liked him very much. I might have admired him a great deal, but I wouldn't necessarily have liked him. However, he said something about the present being the hinge of now. The things that happen now make one realize the importance of now, that now is both in the past and the future. There is always going to be a now in the past and the future.

Ameliasburgh, Ontario, August 8, 1991

ANNE SZUMIGALSKI

It is a chilly November morning in Saskatoon as I ride a borrowed bicycle down from Idylwyld and turn onto the crescent where Anne Szumigalski lives in a brown house built in 1942. On the black metal mailbox, a sign reads: NO FLYERS PLEASE/ SAVE THE TREES. Anne welcomes me, saying, "You must be cold and no gloves." The interview is held in an L-shaped room. On the right, as you enter, is a bookcase with volumes of poetry, including a copy of *Dogstones*. There are shelves of plants across the front window. On one of these is a brown clay angel; next to it is a green carved polar bear. On the wall to the left is a dulcimer. Anne says it's not the one in "Kubla Khan," then recites a few lines. On the wall opposite the window is a bookcase devoted to wildlife and natural history, including books on herbs, mushrooms, and whales. On top of it are tiles painted with various flowers: Indian paintbrush, prairie gentian, cinquefoil, smooth fleabane, and camas. Above it is a self-portrait of her daughter, painted when she was at a girl's private school. "That was when she was involved with her own beauty." There are pictures everywhere on the walls, mostly done by her own family. There is a picture of three men on a bench, in which they appear to have branches growing out of their bodies. In the upper corner of the room is a wasp's nest cradled by an old twisted weed wand. Anne points to the garden observing, "I'm quite a gardener. Jan put in two pools for the children. He brought rocks in from the field when he was surveying." She says there's never enough room for her books, which now lie in piles around the room. "The carpenters are preparing the back room for my study." At the end of the house, beyond the glass doors, they work through the interview putting up the interior wall.

*

I want to ask you a question about your philosophy of poetry. Why is the speculation of poetics so important?

For me it's important. I'm not sure it is for all poets, but I like to speculate. If you read my recent work, you will see that a lot of it is speculation or speculation on a theme, very often a theme on mathematics or on other things that I thought of or ideas, or maybe questions and ideas. That's the way I am; that's the sort of thing I like. I like speculation. I like argument. I like disagreement.

Argument seems to be central to your poetry.

It is. That's central to my thinking. I, of course,

don't demand that everybody else who writes poetry does it that way. In fact, I may read somebody else's poem and think this is a great poem that doesn't have any of those themes or forms, but for myself that's very important when I'm writing.

I noticed a dialectic in the poem, "A House with a Tower," two different parts of yourself.

Yes, we're arguing: the Celtic half of myself and the Anglo-Saxon half of myself. I know at least one side of my family – where they came from and how long they were in Britain – the Anglo-Saxon side back a thousand years when they first came to Britain.

What about the Celtic side?

The Celtic side I know very little about. I only know that my father's people came from Wales. That was just one generation before my father's generation. I have gone back and lived in Wales, so I certainly sympathize with that part of myself more than I do with the Anglo-Saxon side, which is always telling me that I mustn't embroider stories, or that fact is the same as truth, which my Celtic side knows perfectly well is utter nonsense.

So it's important for you to be aware of these different strains of your family.

Well, my Anglo-Saxon side annoys me a lot, but I'm glad it's there because I like to have this conflict that helps me to understand, well, everybody in my family or outside, I think. But this is a completely different idea even now, you see, for an Englishman and a Welshman. They have a different idea of what honour is. An Englishman thinks honour is not telling lies; a Welshman thinks, "Of course people tell lies – all the time, and it's fun," but if you give your word, that's it. You must never go against your word. Well, an Englishman will get round that very easily. It's almost as if he's telling you the facts which he thinks of as the truth.

Do you find that people often erase difference or conflict, when in actual fact they should be celebrating it?

I do agree with that statement, entirely. Of course you should celebrate it. We don't want to all be the same, any more than we all want to speak the same language or have the same culture. Fundamentally, we're all human, but there's quite a variance in that and that's something to celebrate. I have a poem about different languages. I am expressing my admiration for all these different languages and not wanting any of them to die, or to be examined too closely. I think perhaps scholars are too anxious to examine things down to the bone and that even at the bone, they won't find out about everything, but they might think they have.

Can you speak about your family and how they helped you to write?

It's very important to me to be one of seven children because you get slightly neglected. There's no way parents can take notice of seven children all at once or singly. There are times when they are concentrating on one of the other children. Therefore, in spite of the fact that you're surrounded by these children, you get more chance at solitude perhaps than single children, because your mother can't worry if you go off for a walk in the woods. She's got baby twins to look after, so they give you a sort of freedom, which is very exciting. Also, parents with seven children are always hard up unless they're extremely rich, because seven children cost a lot of money to bring up, so that a lot of your amusements are quite simple and a lot of them are writing games or speaking games, reading and so forth. I think that's very good for children; things are too complicated for children now. It's difficult for them to have a chance to be solitary or to make up their own games.

I want to move on to another period in your life, when you worked as a nurse during the Second World War.

When I joined up for the Second World War, I joined up with the British Red Cross. I did some medical work with refugees and I looked after Belgian refugees, but medical things or nursing are not my strong point. I ended up mostly being an interpreter and writing small histories of these people.

Did this affect your later writing?

Probably not. I still wrote a lot of poetry and

other things, but it allowed me to go the way of learning several languages, which I liked very much. And there I learned that after three languages you somehow get an insight into what language really is. I think in schools they don't teach children that. They don't say, "Look, this thing is language, and it has all these branches, but it's all language." No child seems to get taught that. They say, "This is English, this is French, this is German." The root of language is just like mathematics, the same thing, but you never tell small children when they start off: "Look, this is mathematics. This is a system; it's another language. You can do all these things with mathematics." They say, "Well, add up this little sum two, three and six" and so on. A child may get very bored doing that. If only they would teach theory to small children, what things really are. Children who are going forward to think a lot would be much happier, less frustrated. I find that bright children very often give up trying to learn. They get so completely bored with the way they are taught. I'm speaking of myself, too.

You met your husband around this time.

Yes, I met my husband in Germany when I was working with the British Red Cross. We were attached to the army in civilian relief; part of our civilian relief was PWX. These Poles that we were looking after had been prisoners of war. They were actually in the hospital because they had been marched across Germany by the Germans being chased by the Russians. The Germans would rather be caught by the British than by the Russians. So in fact, that's how I met him. And we got married very soon after that. It was a very romantic period of my life.

Yes, for my parents too.

I was writing to people's parents. I'd write letters for them. I'd let their families know where they were. Or, I had to go to the morgue and write to tell their parents that some of them had died. I liked them all, except this one fellow whom I thought was absolutely terrible. That's the man I married. That, I think, shows something about my delight in conflict.

You were talking about your husband and differences.

My husband died some years ago, but while he was alive we were always at loggerheads. We were always arguing about everything, but we couldn't leave each other alone. We never could have left each other because it would have been so boring to be anywhere else. It was a continual sort of argument and talk about this and that. I now find that I don't get on very well with his family, whom I feel slightly responsible for. He was so very different from them and that may be one of the reasons why he was so anxious to come to Canada. The other reason was that, after so many generations of Poles had gone to war, he just didn't want his children to be hauled off to another war and he knew that in Canada they probably wouldn't. There are hardly any Szumigalskis left. There's only three of them in Poland, and us three, myself and my two sons in Canada. That's all the Szumigalskis there are and that's because they have been killed off in wars. He was against war, of course, but he wasn't against the conflict of the mind.

Now, that's what happened to my mother's family. They left Holland because there was a chance it would happen again.

No, you can't let it happen again. "You know, it's got to be broken sometimes," he said. You've got to break this thing where all these young men, and of course, nowadays young women, are slaughtered by wars. And, in fact, out of the small unit which I belonged to, the Civilian Relief No. 1, two of the women were killed: one by a sniper and one taken prisoner. So you can see that actually it was dangerous, interestingly dangerous. And, at certain times of your life, you like danger. I loved it. It sort of brought something up in myself: the response to danger. Excitement. So I understand why people want to go to war. But, I don't want anybody to do it again.

Some people whom I've heard talk about the war said it was the best time of their lives.

I can understand that if they were very young. You have no responsibilities beyond fighting or looking after fighting people. The work we did was civilian relief, so that the army wouldn't have to look after the civilians. We were attached to the Tank

Corps and when they moved over the Rhine, we did too. We looked after any civilians who got hurt or who were in difficulty. That's what we did until we got to Germany when we worked for the military government looking after refugees. And, of course, when we actually got into Germany one of the things we did was to look after people who had been released from concentration camps, go in there and get them out. That had a great influence on me. Only now I'm beginning to write about it. It was buried in my mind for a long time. I'm writing a play about it, a poetic play.

It must have influenced you subconsciously.

It has influenced my whole life. I could not any longer see things the same way as I could before, mostly because of the guilt that you have because you didn't know these things were happening. You were having a jolly time while all these people were being killed and I realized that it happens every decade or so, that this happens again in other parts of the world. If that was the last time, we could have then put it behind us, but it's not. It won't ever be the last time that people want to kill off whole countries or races of people perhaps. And it goes back very far in history: remember Genghis Khan, who killed everybody in a city because they spoke rudely to his soldiers, and then built the walls of the city with their bones and skulls. That's the feeling of despair that I gained at that time. Before that I didn't have this knowledge of this dark side of humanity. That certainly changed my life.

Well, that's there in "Shrapnel."

Yes, of course. It has to be because it's part of myself. I suppose it's part of most people. When I came back from this and I spoke to my parents, I felt older than they were because of seeing and doing these things. Then I felt very old, but of course I wasn't. I wasn't too old to fall madly in love with a Pole anyway. *[Laughter.]*

You immigrated to Canada in 1951.

That's right.

Did you have a difficult time adjusting to life on the prairies?

For a year I had some difficulties. We didn't have a bean so we moved around. My husband had a job at a sodium sulfate mine in the south of the province. I found that extraordinary landscape absolutely terrifying at first, and then it became my home landscape. To tell you how it influenced me, at that time I had two very small children, and I had this thing called "fear of knives." Yes, every night I would try to hide all the sharp knives in the house. I put them in all sorts of places, put them in drawers, in vases, in boxes. In the end I found a drawer with a key, put all the knives in and gave the key to my husband. I had no idea why I was doing this. I just thought I was crazy. After a while I got used to the landscape. I got used to the place. I didn't feel so strange, and the fear of knives just went away.

What did you feel like doing with these knives?

Well, I didn't know until a long time later, but this is not an uncommon thing for young mothers to do. It's a kind of psychological thing. And what it means is: You're afraid you're going to kill your children and yourself, because your mind is terrified. I was really surprised when I heard what it meant; I just thought I was frightened of these knives, that's all. After a year I got used to the prairie and I have absolutely loved it ever since, but it was a very barren landscape, in the south of the province. It wasn't quite flat; it was slightly undulating. It obviously had been the bottom of the sea and had boulders on the rises.

How did you come to love the prairie?

I realized that was the place I was meant to be. I thought to myself I wish I had been born here. I like the landscape. Also, I liked the political landscape which was so much more open and free than I was used to. I haven't been able to let this landscape go, since then. The last time I was in Britain, I was on one of these red buses that run around London. I was sitting beside somebody who asked me where I came from, and I began to cry because I realized that I couldn't stand this place and I wanted to go back to the prairie. And, I thought to myself how ridiculous, this old lady sitting there crying because she's not on the prairie *[laughter]*, but it just gets you, you know. It's more grand than mountains.

And yet your work expresses not an external landscape, but an internal country, un paysage intérieur.

Well, that's quite true. That's exactly what it is.

Paradoxical.

It is. To me, of course, it's exterior as well, but for my work I don't actually write prairie poems about grassland. Every now and again it does come into my poems, like in my poem about the bees where I explain at the end of that poem what I think about flatness. It's always there; so is the space between my poems. It's all I think of as being prairie. That's the only landscape which I want now. I intend to stay here till I rush off to the great prairie in the sky. *[Laughter.]*

I'd like to turn to the question of influence. First of all could you talk about Blake?

I read a lot of poetry when I was a child, but Blake was read to me, the *Songs of Innocence*, before I could read. That formed a very strong background to my feeling. And again, it's something to do with the ambiguity of those forms.

They're very ambiguous.

They're very, very ambiguous and I remember as a child, maybe four years old, I thought it was a physical feeling, this ambiguity.

It's a wonderful experience to have as a child.

Yes, absolutely. My mother was great for reading aloud. Later on, she read us a lot of novels, but when we were little children she read us poems and so forth. I don't remember her ever reading children's books to us; we read those later on when we were a little older, but they were mostly poems and then a lot of classical novels. That really influenced me, that idea of ambiguity and that landscape of the mind, imagination, the vision. Since then I thought that poetry must have this great imagining vision and insight and that is the internal landscape.

Who were the poets who influenced you?

It's very difficult for me to think of all of them. One of them was James Joyce. One doesn't think of him perhaps as a poet, but he was, and I remember going about, hopping from foot to foot and saying to myself:

> Lean out of the window,
> Golden-hair,
> I hear you singing
> A merry air.
>
> My book was closed
> I read no more,
> Watching the fire dance
> On the floor.

I don't think I've read that poem since, but I remember it from my childhood. I was always doing that, you know. I spent a lot of time talking to myself. I do that still. People now think it's because I'm old, but it isn't. I've done it forever. Later on I got influenced "of course" by Baudelaire. I think you can see in my work as well, the influence of young Wordsworth.

You have an affinity with Wordsworth.

A lot of people have noticed that and I have too. One of the things is this wandering in a landscape and writing poems which don't always look like an external landscape, but like the internal country. Also, both Blake and Wordsworth have this sort of idea of childhood as some glorious thing. You can quote either of them on this, and I think if you are a child or if you're older, you look back on this as a golden thing, a time when you had time to think. When you start learning things and have to keep up with your schoolwork, it means you don't have that great time when you were four-ish and could think as long as you liked.

Do you read literary criticism?

Yes, I do. I sometimes translate it into English as I read along. It's quite hard, though. I think if these people were to learn to write straightforward, really well expressed English, everybody would understand them better. They'd be able to get their points across, and their books would be about half the size. Maybe that wouldn't be a good thing; nobody would think they were doing anything. We don't have enough criticism in Canada. We don't have enough good criticism, literary criticism. We are stuck in some theories that are really a little bit old now, growing long white beards, and we can't get out of them.

What do you think of new theories like structuralism and deconstruction?

Well, that's what I mean, deconstruction has been going on perhaps a little long. And of course, it's great that it really is a French theory and I like French. But isn't it time we moved forward? Literary theory should come out of people's writing, not be something that somebody thinks of and people will write to. It never has been like that before. If you look back and you see the people writing about writing or writing about literature, you'll see they're writing about something that's already obviously there. But nowadays, I think people are inventing these theories and hoping that we're all going to write to this pattern, and we're not. I mean that's the sort of thing that puts my back up, so I wouldn't dream of taking the slightest notice of them, for that reason. From there to there to there.

How does a poem begin for you?

I don't know that because I think I do a lot of work subconsciously, but how it appears in my conscious mind is as a phrase which I play around with. I think to myself: "This is a poem-phrase." I don't know what the poem is about. I just know the phrase because I am so much influenced by language. This is the difficult part, to decide when to bring that phrase out and write it down. You have to wait until you think the poem is ready. Then when you write it down and it all comes out, you say, "Oh, that's what it's about." That's what happens to me, but then I work a lot on my poems afterwards. I may do thirty different versions of it before I'm finished.

There is a certain kind of attention you need before you can write a poem.

Yes, that's good. That's what you feel, and if you misjudge, that's when it doesn't work.

Do you see writing as a physical act?

Yes I do, and I hardly ever write anything but letters in longhand. When I was twelve or thirteen my father gave me a little typewriter because he thought if I was going to be a writer I might as well have one. And ever since then, I have always wanted to type. Or in this case, now, we don't type anymore, but it's the same thing because I like to see the length of the line and it's much easier when you type than when you have handwriting.

I sometimes hold the poem up to the lamp to see what it looks like.

Yes, it doesn't always look right, does it? I don't think you can divide those things up, the look and the sound of it. Both have to be right. So I don't think you can say, "Well, this looks great, but it doesn't sound right."

Do you pay much attention to punctuation and line breaks?

I am usually now writing my poems almost as prose, so the breaks are in the middle sometimes, rather than at the edges. Punctuation, I think, is the most difficult part of writing poetry. Whatever decision you make it's not like punctuating prose because you do have line breaks, which is punctuation in itself. Should you put in all these little commas . . . should you put in nothing? I've tried all sorts of ways, and I think I've conquered several of them, but I want to try something else. At the moment I'm punctuating all of my poems as though they were prose because they are in prose form. But I haven't always done that, even in that form, so every time I start on a new manuscript, I make up my mind how I'm going to punctuate it. I try out different things because I think that's one of the most difficult things to get exactly as I want it. It never is exactly as I want it.

You have been writing prose poems.

I've written a lot, yes. I still write poems with line breaks too.

How is a prose poem different than other poems?

It's different because the rhythm of a prose sentence is different from the poetic rhythm. There is a prose rhythm in it. On the other hand, it must have all the elements of poems, the use of images, the fact that it's compressed. The sound of the language is very important, even if it has a slightly different rhythm. And it must have some kind of poetic insight, end like a poem. It's a poem, but it admits of another rhythmical English. When looking at things like blank verse, one sees it is not very different from the poetic rhythm, but it's slightly different. The ending is different.

The prose poem has become a very popular form.

Yes. I think it belongs to our times, but of course, it's been here before. It comes in and out like other forms. We always think we've invented a new form, but we haven't.

You use a number of different points of view. Why is point of view so important to you?

I used to write plays when I was younger and I'm starting to write plays again. I have this idea of there being more than one voice speaking, and I think it's very seldom my "I" voice; I don't use that very often. Even when I put "I" in a poem, it's not necessarily my voice. I also, as you probably notice, like to have male and female voices. Sometimes I think the music of the spheres is a motet.

"Victim" has an unusual point of view, the point of view of a murdered girl, inside the pocket of the murderer.

That's right. My sympathies are with the murdered girl. I could not have written that poem in the voice of the murderer. I might have done in a simply impersonal voice, but I don't think it would be so effective there. I think it's really important for this play, as it might be termed a play, to be played out as a monologue by the person who's been murdered. When you think of it, it's quite possible on the stage to do that. That's probably the connection with drama.

Some of your poems are concerned with violence, for example, violence against women as in "Victim" or violence against men as in "Shrapnel." Why is there so much violence in your work?

There is so much violence in life. I don't think that's something we can ignore. Human nature is very violent. We'd all probably like there to be less violence in us, but it is there, so I think I have to express it. It is positive as well as negative because violence is energy. That energy of young people, especially young males, has been harnessed all through history to make them warriors.

That's in the poem "Shrapnel."

Yes. I see this fellow as being caught in this thing. He's been a warrior for eons, but . . .

. . . but he changes before he dies.

Yes, well, faced with death one might as well realize that there is a possibility that this violence couldn't be like death. I once became very aware of this fact when I saw an illustration of Homer, and the illustration was of a soldier, probably from the Second World War, lying with his helmet still on, with his head in the Mediterranean, the water washing over it. What difference is there? It's still part of people's nature. I mean, we try to bend this in various ways, but can we? Is that the natural thing? If we were animals, like tigers, we would be violent too and that would be the good part of us because that's what the life of a tiger is. Is the life of a human necessarily violent, I'm asking. Is my female desire to get that expunged a mistaken idea? What can we do with it?

There are strong feminist concerns in your work, as in the poem "Disk," and many others. Do you consider yourself a feminist?

That's a question I get asked a lot. I think I'm a "womanist." I'm not sure I even like the word "feminism." It sounds both violent and frilly at the same time. I'd rather think of myself as female than feminine, and I'd rather think of myself as a woman, than as a sort of female activist. I don't know, but I think, "Of course I'm a woman, of course I'm a feminist," if somebody likes to express it like that. There is no other way, right? Somebody who's brought up in a family where there are boys and girls and, a fairly long time ago, can't possibly mistake the fact that all around you are these things – boys are being treated differently from girls. They're educated differently, different things expected of them. And that's something that used to make me very annoyed when I was a girl. So I suppose I am a feminist.

Yet you have been very critical of some aspects of contemporary feminism.

I think what I am critical of is a sort of violence. I think the mistake of feminists is to try and make themselves not into feminists *[laughter]* but into "masculinists" if you see what I mean. I don't want to pick up those things which I don't particularly care for in the male. I don't want that. I want to be wholly and absolutely a woman, and I very much like being a woman. I find it really difficult to whine about it. And, the fight which I've had all my life, as all women have, to "make myself heard" and so forth, I quite enjoyed, as a matter of fact. I sometimes think that if I believed in the transmigration of souls that I would think this has been my only chance to be a woman, and I'm making the most of it because I really like it. I like being a mother. I like having the female point of view, and I like being able to argue with the male point of view, whether it's in myself as we all have both in us, or with my husband, with whom I had this many long years of argument; he was a very strongly masculine person. I liked that about him. I didn't want to change him to be more in my way of thinking and I'm sure he didn't really want to change me. I think being a woman doesn't mean that you are totally spunkless and don't fight; I think it means you do fight. Women have always fought against this thing. I think traditionally perhaps women have been too patient; I believe in female impatience I'd say. And I will always feel like that. The other thing, which I have a very strong feeling for – perhaps that makes me a feminist – is that I like the feeling of being able to hand down my female genes into other generations. I have only one grandchild and it's a female. I am absolutely delighted with this, because I know that there are things that I couldn't hand down in the male line, that I could only hand down in the female line, and that is absolutely a physical fact. They know that now. Women have always known that. There's this female thing; you hand it down and I want my granddaughter to have a daughter so that we can hand this down and it won't ever be lost. I was brought up in a family of five girls and only two boys. My mother was the strong partner in my parents' marriage, so you can see how I had this very strong female feeling. Does that make me feminist or not? I don't know. As I said, what I don't like about feminism is its propensity to whine; I don't like that. "Kick, don't whine," I'd say. If you don't like something, put on some very pointed shoes and give them a damn good kick. Don't hang around whining about what people have done to you.

Your poems are filled with elephants, foxes, dogs, bees and beetles, a veritable cosmic zoo. [Laughter.]

Well, the cosmic zoo and of course the cosmic flora which I go in for is because that's one of my great interests, natural history. If I have other interests besides literature, one of them is certainly the natural sciences, from botany to physics. It's very mysterious to me whether or not the material world, or particularly the biosphere, is an image of something, or if the philosophical side is an image of that material side. Like Blake, I haven't really worked this out yet. So I'm very much aware of all the other beings in the world. And I strongly feel that plants are as much alive as any kind of animal.

You were always interested in creating languages; you, in fact, create a fox language in "Fennec."

Yes, a written language. Lately I have become very interested in written languages as apart from spoken languages. I think you read my last book. You will notice that there's a couple of essays or pieces in that which are posing this question. Is it possible that before a spoken language we could have had a written language? And, I probably think the answer to that is no, but I want to explore these possibilities and I am exploring this possibility at the moment. Before we opened our mouths to speak, and before perhaps we can speak, we have to have the proper equipment. The chimpanzees have all the other equipment, but they can't speak because their throats aren't the right shape. Before that, did we know a language, and did we express it in signs or scratches or words?

I am curious about the foxes. Why are there so many foxes in your poems?

I've always been very interested in foxes; I like foxes, but in each of my books I had not known until

I got the whole book together that I was so interested in one image. In a certain book there are more foxes than other things. In other books, there are inanimate things like a lot of wires and strings, but the fox has always been a very interesting image, a very interesting animal: not a dog, quite right, a mysterious animal. When I was a child we lived in the country and opposite us was a sort of desolate little patch of stony ground over which the foxes used to mate when they were in their mating season. I would sit up on the back of my bed because I could hear this woman crying. They sound so much like women when they're in heat and are calling the dog fox. I thought this mysterious life going on which sounds so human, but is not, is more mysterious. Right under my window. It took a lot of convincing. Everybody told me, well that's just the vixen. You know she's in heat and she's calling the fox. I didn't believe that at first; I thought they were people, so I think maybe I think still, in a way, foxes are people.

And then, you have the poem where the mother gives birth to the fox.

Yes, exactly. People. Is it a child, a fox, or not, as the case may be? Or is something wild in us akin to the fox?

Dogstones *is the title of a collection of your poems. What is the origin of that?*

Well, it's the plant that illustrates it. It's called dogstones. If you look at the plant, you'll see this orchid. It looks like the sexual organs of a dog. That's why it's called Dogstones, I mean, the root of the plant. There are other plants called goatstones. They all belong to the same family.

Dog also is a reverse of "God."

Of course, but that comes out better in my story about the dog when he's deciding whether or not he's a human or whether he's a superhuman or subhuman.

Do you consider yourself a religious person?

Yes, I think. I'm not sure if I'm a religious person, but I'm definitely a religious poet. I mean, that kind of feeling comes into all my work, but I'm not attached to any particular religion, though I'm very interested in all of them. I do quite a lot of studying in theology, not only Christian theology but others because I find that part of humans very interesting. It's really interesting how people see whatever deities they worship and how important that is to them. One of my thoughts is that we have imagined gods with enough imagination to imagine us imagining them. We all are imagined beings. If that's a religious statement, then I am a very religious person.

Saskatoon, Saskatchewan, November 12, 1992

JAMES REANEY

The approach to the University of Western Ontario is one of the most pleasant in the country. You can see the contours of the old golf course on which the campus is built. The limestone buildings are a modified Gothic style. This morning there are a number of summer school students strolling to class. The office of James Reaney is in the tower of University College. Along the dark oak framed walls, there are posters of "La Belle Province" and theatre announcements that haven't been changed since the days I was an undergraduate. On the third floor I pass the humming of machinery, walk down a corridor which overlooks a stage where there's a children's drama workshop. On the stained glass windows are the symbols of harp, castle and ship.

James Reaney has just returned from photocopying a script with a musical score. The large tower room is about sixteen feet high. Posters of Reaney's plays hang on the wall: *Gyroscope, Wacousta, Sticks and Stones, Handcuffs, The St. Nicholas Hotel, King*

Whistle! and *The Shivaree*. The room is dominated by a ten foot long desk on which, James explains, are materials related to the Donnellys: a long row of index cards, old photographs of the houses and inhabitants of Lucan, notebook binders filled with Biddulphiana, a scrapbook of Donnelly material. On the shelves beside the desk on the west wall are the little magazines – runs of *Northern Review*, *Gants du Ciel*, *First Statement*, *Brick*, *Here and Now*, *Alphabet*, *ellipse*, the Indian File Books.

We sit on a green couch for the interview. On the wall facing us there is a painting by a pupil of Reaney's, of The Nihilist Spasm Band. Above us is a picture, "A Well Organized Athletic Meet on Centre Island, 1907 two women carrying eggs on a spoon." Above those are topographical maps representing Grand Bend, St. Mary's and Stratford.

*

You spend much of your time up at your farm near Stratford.

Yes, that's right. You've been there too, Laurence. I was born there. That's my region, and I get a lot of ideas from it. I get some of my best ideas from the garden. I think when you're brought up on a farm you get used to doing a lot of work and your mind tends to wander while you're doing this repetitive work, you know, stooping and hoeing turnips. The mind does tend to wander and your hands are very satisfied with physical work so your mind can sort of flower. Unlike the French Revolution histories, it didn't seem to deaden my mind, although I did notice cases of deadened minds around me.

Another fascinating feature of your farm is the geology and history.

Yes. I've dug up, accidentally, flint scrapers and a stone axe head and had them analyzed down at the Royal Ontario Museum. They're three thousand years old and you realize that the landscape three thousand years ago was more like tundra with great big stands of Jack Pine and hunting people that went through Palaeo-Indians, Woodland people.

You decode the land like a language.

The thing that opened my eyes to what it was all about was a book by Putnam called *Physiography of Southern Ontario*. That was the first book that helped me to understand what the landscape was like. Everyone just said, "Well it's flat," but it isn't. It's actually not until you get down to Windsor where it really is flat. Even there it's shaped by glaciers and sand deposits, all with Gaelic names such as kames and eskers and drumlins, from the original physiographer who was an Ulsterman.

From 1944–1948 you were an undergraduate at the University of Toronto. There were other writers there at the time: Margaret Avison, Robert Weaver, Colleen

Thibaudeau. What was the university like for a young writer?

Well, it was very good for a young writer in a certain way. I was at University College which was dominated by the history of ideas approach, as interpreted by Professor Arthur Woodhouse. That was not good for poetry. Woodhouse seemed to think that John Milton first had some wonderful ideas which all seemed to be in the catechism that fifty thousand kids studied at school at the time. I think poetry doesn't work like that. Philosophy and theology are its enemies, not its friends. So that wasn't so good. But, on the other hand, each college had its own publication. We had *The Undergrad*. It was beautifully designed by a young returned veteran called Paul Arthur who runs his own design company now. He really encouraged people. So did Robert Weaver who was editor of it for one year. Colleen Thibaudeau, Phyllis Gotlieb, and myself were University College poets and we were all cheek by jowl in Peggy Atwood's anthology. We were in the same year, you see. They were very healthy influences to have because Colleen had super sharp training from her father who was a French teacher. Phyllis Gotlieb, you know, just knew tons about Hasidism and she became a science fiction writer. It was very good to have literary friends like that who also wrote. Then Victoria College was another hotbed of poetry. Margaret Avison was a recent graduate. We got to be friends with her because my wife to be, Colleen Thibaudeau, wrote one of the very first theses on modern Canadian Literature at U. of T.

Have you had an interest since then in French Canadian poetry?

Yes. Dr. Gael Turnbull (a medical doctor, not the more boring kind), a friend of John Sutherland, published a series in about 1948 including Alain Grandbois, Saint-Denys-Garneau, and so on. I don't think they had the French. I think they just had the English. It opened my eyes, for example, when you got a poet saying, "the skunk, the cathedral censer of the woods." No one in Ontario thinks that way. *[Laughter.]* Saint-Denys-Garneau's houses are quite different from my concept of a farmhouse and there are terrible traps in him, you know, with the Jansenist vision and all the rest of it.

You had a reputation of being a kind of enfant terrible.

Because of the short story, yes, "The Box Social," that was published in *Liberty*. That caused terrible kerfuffles and, as a result, I didn't get to be editor of *The Undergrad*. Anyway, they didn't want an editor who could publish a story that horrifying, which made me pause and think that there is something the matter around here. I notice in my diary for the period I am saying, "Don't they understand there is such a thing as Neo-Gothic." You see, Robert Weaver, who was the person who made that decision, thought that William Faulkner was a realist.

Well, he is in some of his stories, but "A Rose for Miss Emily" is not a realist story. I just don't get it. It's Southern Gothic. Peggy Atwood recently taught a course called Ontario Gothic. I was trying rather early in the scene . . . the old dark farmhouse and the horrors therein. But, remember, this story was first published in *The Undergrad* when edited by Paul Arthur. He didn't seem to admire Ontario Gothic.

Was First Statement *too early for you?*

Just a shade. I never knew all the ins and outs of that until Colleen started doing her thesis, but evidently there were two or three rival groups in the anglophone poetry situation in Montreal. They never seemed to talk to any French Canadian poets. They were in their own little McGill bubble. *Preview* was run by P.K. Page and Frank Scott. And then there were breakoffs with things like *First Statement* and *Northern Review* with Irving Layton and John Sutherland reviewing Robert Finch's poems savagely, for example, when he got the Governor General's Award. I never even saw a copy of *First Statement* until about 1947. But *Northern Review* would have been here in Toronto. Colleen was the local editor who distributed the books. *Northern Review* was a big influence on us because Colleen and I were published in it. Then we went down to Montreal to interview John Sutherland, A.M. Klein, and all the local poets for Colleen's thesis, while Sutherland was bringing out other things on his press, Irving Layton for example. Irving Layton's poems of that period were noteworthy for such images as "church spires like hemorrhoids on the city's anus." *[Laughter.]* Imagine being exposed to that at the age of nineteen.

With your particular aesthetic would you have a closer affinity with one of these magazines?

No one talked like that then because no one could successfully define what literary criticism was, not even Arthur Woodhouse. Frye could, but we didn't hear from him over it, across the park. So you didn't have any role models. What they wanted you to write like was to be very clear, and if you wanted to, probably the impetus was that you wrote about landscape. You weren't supposed to write about vicious problems like orphanages and so on. You'd be amazed at how absolutely quiet the English Department was at University College, re: what poetry really was. You had to find it all out for yourself. One of the really great things to do was not to take modern poetry at University College because that just got you writing like T.S. Eliot. So I never took it. I very gingerly read *The Wasteland*, so as a result, you may appear to have an original style because you have read Auden or Eliot.

You and Colleen had connections with Alan Crawley and CV1.

You see that was another poetry magazine you could publish in. It was just a mimeographed magazine, but somehow or other the design of it was just right and we felt proud to be in it. Mind you, neither Alan Crawley nor John Sutherland were too sure what poetry was or what criticism was, despite the fact that a very fine poet like Earl Birney obviously knew. For example, he shows you how a tradition like Anglo-Saxon poetry can be used with great effect in this country because Canada is very much like Anglo-Saxon England. As Frye has pointed out, you've got the same kind of haunted wilderness and sudden ghost towns that could have been founded by rodents. *[Laughter.]* All of this eventually comes out more clearly in my magazine called *Alphabet*.

What were the circumstances in which you met Colleen Thibaudeau?

In class. I was in class with her for four years and we were friends long before we fell in love. I can't really say when I actually met her. She just was in class and we still have a circle of friends that are from that class. We did all meet, the whole four college bunch of us, at the college where we took these things called Greek and Latin Literature, absolute torture courses that were given each year, you know, one year on satire, the next year on tragedy. We had McLuhan around too. McLuhan was just starting to be an influence, and Harold Innis was also very important.

Did you have any personal dealings with either?

McLuhan, yes. Colleen and I babysat for him. He

had a huge family. You know, I met Frye in a radio station thing ... a panel discussion on conversation. I went to some Frye church lectures. Harold Innis was just a person I saw walking around campus.

The Stratford Festival was founded in 1952.

Right, and that made a big difference. We got married in 1951. It got started in 1952 and we saw the first season. Breakthrough. What a breakthrough to see Shakespeare properly done. They didn't sort of crawl around the top of the poetry. They simply let the poetry fall where it might. And you saw how the plays worked, whereas the Canadian productions of Shakespeare had always been so careful about the poetry. You thought you were reading it, you know.

This must have been a turning point for you.

Yes, the big difference it made to Canadian productions was shoes. Finally you saw the proper shoes they should be wearing. Evidently it was the person who makes the shoes for the Ukrainian Dance Ensemble who made the shoes for the Shakespeare Festival – you know, medieval shoes, and things like that. Actually, I'm not that fussy about the shoes being right *[laughter]*, but it was fun to see them because you had no idea what they used to wear in Shakespeare productions. Oh, Malabar's idea of a shoe. Malabar is a costume agency. But the big breakthrough was, as somebody says in their book on poetic drama, "the poetic drama is not an end in itself; it's the archetypal design inside that Shakespeare . . . the dynamics of that that are important," just the way Guthrie had them speak the poetry (he's from Northern Ireland). That's why I think he worked in Canada very well. He'd been here before, Tyrone Guthrie, doing drama for the CNR which organized the original prototype *[ha ha ha]* of the CBC. And by the way, speaking of my ten years teaching Creative Writing at Manitoba, Andre Nault stopped the Ontario surveyors dead in their tracks because they were putting straight lines across his hay privilege. That's where the bus turned into Fort Garry, but no one at the University of Manitoba ever talked about it. They were very blind to their own history all this time until I found blind historian Margaret Macleod, who told me tons. She put me onto Pierre Falcon whom I translated when I was there. He was the first Manitoba balladeer and the first real poet in Canada besides David Willson at Sharon. In 1815 he was writing songs that everyone knew on the prairies.

History is an integral part of your own poetry.

The awful thing that happened to history in education in Ontario is that it was made into social studies, which is the whore of Babylon as far as I'm concerned. It devastated the States too. There was one very good thing that people said about it. It made tots into sociologists. You were taught sociology. You did your own county, for example. You didn't have to worry about York and Upper Canada anymore; that larger history wouldn't be important so far as they were concerned.

There's been a report that the government is thinking of changing the counties.

They've already done that. They've done that with Lincoln County. Lincoln County is now part of Niagara, bigger than Niagara Falls. I think that's a mistake, an utter mistake. But they can't do that in the States, evidently. The county system is written right into the Constitution and, as a result, you get a different feeling about the States. Faulkner's so great, you see, on Yoknapatawpha County.

When you are teaching Canadian poetry, it's essential to explain counties, townships, lots, concession lines.

A lot of people don't know about that despite the regional project emphasis in education. At education conferences people generally say, "Well, we don't live like that anymore." Well, okay but you look at Shakespeare dramas. You could easily say to Shakespeare, "We don't live like that anymore." Why are you putting on a play about King Lear? "We don't live like that anymore." Well, what do you want me to write about, apartment buildings? Yes, that's important. It is important. But the apartment buildings grew out of this other past thing, you know.

Those apartment buildings were built on top of barns which were built on certain concession lines and in cer-

tain townships. The scene has changed, but the names and the language of the whole place is still there.

The road grid business still goes on. So I don't know.

Much has been written about Frye's influence on you. However, you didn't take a course with him until you came back from Manitoba to work on your PhD.

This is much froth. You get people with nincompoop ideas about what an influence is. I think it was too late for him to have an influence on me. The big influences were the Bible, and the farm, and the Rodeheaver Victory hymn book and so on. Of course Frye gets you interested in symbols and myths and he gives you a terrific conceptual framework, but it's not necessarily going to be that simple to talk about. I think in writing *The Donnellys* I've certainly learned a lot about dramaturgy from Frye, unconsciously. And I've used his ideas in my children's workshops, workshops for young people. But it's no big deal. You get the same thing from T.S. Eliot and the same thing from reading Dante that you get from him, and the same thing from William Blake. And William Blake I really think had a revolutionary influence on Frye.

William Blake was an influence on your early work. In fact, in the first editorial of Alphabet *you quoted Richard Stingle's quotation of* The Marriage *of* Heaven and Hell.

Right. Well, one of the things that I did, the same

thing that Freud did, that I suddenly realized that no one had ever been able to explain at University College was explain why Keats used myths. Why? We don't live like that anymore. Well, of course, what Freud pointed out was that people are still influenced by Venus and they are still very heavily influenced by Oedipus and so on. These stories, in other words, are inner psychic things and it's the same thing in Blake, only he makes up new names for them, the various parts of God that inhabit people; generally though, in poetry it's a classical myth, so that's sort of fascinating. A lot of people don't like Frye and they are so sure, but they're still on a romantic kick. You get two opposing schools of poetry. You'll always get people who say that poetry is about life and you'll always get people like myself who say that poetry *is* life and to my mind poets should know a thing or two. If you look at the personal life of most poets, particularly the ones that just write about their lives, it's horrendously boring, you know. The Whitman school is still going strong and it will always be there. They've got a thing or two on their side, however.

Dudek and other writers have suggested that myth takes the writer away from life.

You see that's just what I said about Freud. It gets you right back into life. And if it does, then psychoanalysis is such an interesting tool for making people's lives even more disturbed. Why is an Adolf Hitler explained as an anti-Christ figure if mythology is so remote from life? When you see a stupid Hollywood film like the Darth Vader one, it seems to be talking about something that people want to know about, you know, Tolkien? *[Laughter.]* But, I personally find the William Carlos Williams thing a bit restricting. I wish Eliot had stayed in St. Louis. That would have been sort of fascinating, but I can see why he left.

Getting your PhD in two years must have been something of a record.

Yes, there was only one other person who did it. You just have to get some scotch tape and lots of paper and put it together. I had an ideal topic, the "Influence of Spenser on Yeats," given to me by Frye. No one had taken it up and he had been carting it around for years and it introduced me to some symbol mad poets. I had a lot of fun with it.

There is a strong connection between your work and your teaching.

Well, one of the reasons for taking the PhD was to get some sort of framework going for my poetry. *The Red Heart* runs into all kinds of cul-de-sac problems which needed critical help and I wasn't getting it. You see, Peggy Atwood approached Frye and said, "You know I need some advice. I am going to become a waitress and learn about life." He said, "No, you're not. You're going to go off to Harvard. I'll get you a fellowship." That she eventually did. She was working on a thesis on Rider Haggard, whom I was very interested in. In *Alphabet*, you see, she's got a big article on Rider Haggard just before *Listen to the Wind* was written. One of the things people can't understand is that poetry can be dramatic and it needn't necessarily be something you read on the page. It could be oral and might involve the body and the other things that you do in drama. The League of Canadian Poets doesn't know how to deal with that. That organization needs a bat over the head with a broom soaked in whiskey. *[Laughter.]* You get these poets who tell you what the poem means before they read it. Anyway, when you tell people you took a PhD to help you to write poetry, people's mouths fall open. Oh that would kill every bit of poetry in me. Well, good, I wish you would try it . . . is what I can think of saying.

Let's move onto the poetry. The Red Heart *expresses some strong elements of Ontario Gothic. Other Canadian poets, such as Margaret Atwood and Al Purdy, have Gothic elements in their work. What do you mean by Gothic?*

Well, it's all explained in a book by Jay Macpherson who's part of a group of people that I met when I was at graduate school, along with Peggy Atwood, by the way, who was just a freshwoman at that point. It's the spirit in solitude, the isolated person rattling around, usually in an old dark castle in the early Gothic novels, but then in Faulkner in an old plantation house. In Ontario we can't afford to build plantation houses so we have a farmhouse or an apartment building that has a lot of empty rooms in it, as in *Edible Woman*, and it's a story where, "I'm here because I'm here . . . and I'm going to kill you." It's Snow White and the Seven Dwarfs' time. It's filled with the nightmare of life, but it's this isolation that is at the bottom of it, I think, that comes about because of science. The whole Gothic tradition is already in *Hamlet*.

I think the D.B. Weldon Library on a dark night looks a bit like Elsinore.

It is, yes. English Department life is very Gothic. You could see why Gothic would be attractive. One of the first novels I read was Rider Haggard's *Dawn*. I lived in an old farmhouse and the neighbourhood was filled with strange material, the strangest of which was the Donnelly story.

How did you first come across the Donnellys?

Well, the hired man told me the story when I was about eight and he was from a Catholic settlement area, Ellice Township, north of Stratford where some of the vigilante families arrived afterwards. I heard about it before Thomas Kelley's book came out. And it happened only twenty-five miles away. So it's part of the local folklore.

In your next books, A Suit of Nettles *and* Twelve Letters to a Small Town, *there is a greater freedom, a celebration of life, as well as more advanced poetic techniques.*

A Suit of Nettles was a big experimental book to see what I could do with Renaissance metrics and Renaissance forms. I was fascinated by the idea of *The Shepherd's Calendar* which Adele Wiseman gave me. She was taking it from Malcolm Ross at the time. It's a book that's been deeply complained about as being unreadable and difficult. I don't see that actually. It's an experimental book. *Twelve Letters* was written for the composer John Beckwith. A lot of these poems were read over the radio. *A Suit of Nettles* was read on *Anthology* and so was *Twelve Letters to a Small Town,* with its new format of music, poetry, collage. I did quite a few of those with Beckwith. At this time I was also experimenting with a *One Man Masque*, which was a one-man show that went through the cycles of this world and the other world, the purgatorial world according to Yeats' *A Vision.* It was a lot of fun to do that and I was working on operas with John Beckwith. So there's a lot of technical things going on. *Twelve Letters*, one of my most successful poetry books, has been anthologized this way and that. I could relax. I knew how to handle local material without getting into cul-de-sacs anymore.

What about other Canadian writers that you have been interested in?

I began to be very interested in Canadian literature simply through trying to find a tradition. Originally, when I was out in Manitoba, I felt so benighted that I couldn't seem to find anything. I had Scottish ancestors and there was a big Scottish nationalist movement. I joined that and I remember subscribing to something called *The Saltire Review*. Oh, I burnt my fingers there. It was dull, dull, dull. But then suddenly I got interested in Isabella Valancy Crawford. I actually bought her *Collected Poems* which were still for sale at Ryerson Press. I mean fifty years ago they were published and they still hadn't sold out. I think I got it for a quarter. I sort of got fascinated by her.

It was a bargain.

It was the bargain. Her imagery was darn good. And she used big images, you know.

Native imagery.

A mixture of Indian legend and all that. Then, of course, no one taught Canadian literature at Manitoba. I remember this cruel, cruel scene where they were finally getting together something for the MA students. There were about one and a half of them. They decided that they should get little lectures on what they should know for the generals. I was asked to talk about Canadian poetry and I had written something for a German magazine on Pratt and Grove. I had read all of Frederick Philip Grove in an attempt to find a Manitoba tradition. Lord, a realist and a liar, but anyway ... A person that came ahead of me, a Leavisite told them, "Professor Reaney wants to talk to you about Canadian literature, but there isn't any so you can leave now." That roused my ire and I got going. I've had a lot of fun teaching CanLit.

How about recent Canadian writers?

I really liked Jay Macpherson. I found that when *The Boatman* came out there was a terrific change in my life. Atwood, Macpherson, and myself all do drawings, as well as poems and she (Macpherson) had a set of drawings that I published in *Alphabet*. By this time I had started *Alphabet* which was heavily devoted to Frye, the documentary myth idea which I'd used already in my Creative Writing course and which I thought up myself. It's really the principle of displacement. I liked Macpherson very much. I liked Isabella Valancy Crawford. Margaret Avison I liked very much. I liked Atwood's novels when they started to come out and her new poetry. I liked Emily Carr very much. I liked Garneau, Panneton *(Thirty Acres)* and so on. I began to really get interested in drama and to find the dramatic tradition in Canada.

Back in London you founded Alphabet. *In fact, the first editorial was printed in Manitoba. Could you describe the genesis of this magazine?*

Well, I had decided, in teaching creative writing, that you took a fairy tale and modernized it. Frye would call that displacement: that is, take the Robber Bridegroom and translate it into Manitoba or Winnipeg terms. I had a class of ninety-eight creative writing students at night school, all of whom did this. You'd hear their stories and people would say, "Where's your trip through the forest" and so on. Well, it struck me as I was listening to a paper at the Graduate English Club of which I was the president. I had sixteen papers, sixteen meetings and we met all those graduate English students, some of them over eighty and you know, they were deeply suspicious of Frye and archetypes and very into the history of ideas. One student, a friend of mine, Hope Arnett Lee, listened with me to a paper by Jay Macpherson on Narcissus. She wrote a little essay for *Alphabet* called "Girl in the Mirror" because her experience of being a twin was that you were constantly with a mirror reflection. And it means that you can pass your algebra test with flying colours because your sister's mind, even though she is in another room, is telling you the answers. How about that eh, from mythology? But also this mirror reflection. I put the two things together, Narcissus and Twins, as the first issue of *Alphabet*. And it seemed to me that that was it. We had the Twins documentary which was quite easy to write, and then we had the mythological thing, not so easy to write, but you kept throwing these things at the readers. They might learn a thing or two if they thought about it.

Toward the end of Alphabet's *run you became more open to other forms of poetry; you talk about the Beatles and art, what was happening in London and Vancouver and other parts of the country.*

My own life was reflected in that. I was very

proud of the issue on concrete poetry, edited by Jane Shen; she found a Chinese student to write the big essay on concrete poetry. It seemed to be definitive. The Chinese have a special "in" because of the ideograph. I liked some of the people that came forward with the idea for a myth like the horoscope lady who did a horoscope on her husband, and the fine arts professor who did the thing that went along with horoscope. She had just realized that the Bosch paintings are all about astrology, the reason that people are placed in these strange relationships in those Hieronymus Bosch things. They're astrological allegories, that sort of thing. Many poets believe in constant novelty, the avant-garde; no, no – I believe in the archaic. So I am saying, "Well, I think you should have a look at medieval symbolism, for example, in the horoscope issue or realize that concrete poetry is connected to Chinese poetry and also take a look at the books that come in for review, some of them high brow academic, but of interest to a poet." I was continually being terrorized by the learned presses which had very few outlets for their books. They would send me these difficult books and I'd get them reviewed. Then people would say, "Oh what's that doing in there. This is not avant-garde." So what? You know, you should be more eclectic as a poet and try to take the past under control, as well as the latest things. I get a bit tired of poets constantly yapping about themselves.

Canadian poets will return to myth because, if you

move back to the earth or if you strengthen your regional ties, you will uncover a mythology.

It's there in language. Irving Layton used to go screaming mad about it, "Ah you're using myths all the time." Well, Irving, it's in language, Edward Sapir, for example, his book called *Language*.

Well, Irving Layton is also a mythological poet.

Yes, I know, but try and tell him that. There's two Irving Laytons. There's the real Ezra Pound that writes good poetry and then there's the Ezra Pound who's fascist. It seems to be the weirder the persona, the better the poetry quite often.

You founded the Listeners' Workshop. Children have always been central to your work, not only in your poems which are often written from the child's perspective, but also in your own drama which is centred around them.

This is partially the result of having a family. When you have children you begin to be interested in putting on plays for them and getting them interested in poetry. It's really the whole business of *Alphabet* in terms of the body and oral things, and dance and ballet. So my plays are generally based on children's games. That kind of thing in a play where you have an archetypal shape that is done with the bodies and with the way they walk about on stage is like the Robber Bridegroom story which then has these other things on top of it. That was fascinating. Peggy

Atwood once said that's new, you know, that's something different.

The MacIntyre Building on Talbot Street housed the Alpha Centre and the Alphabet Press, as well as an excellent poetry series which I recall.

We also had a film series and brought in a lot of American and Canadian avant-garde films. Jack Chambers ran it. Alpha Centre was a very ambitious organization. I got a lot of help, but I couldn't get anybody to take it over. It just involved a hell of a lot of work, but it was fun. This was just before the grant system got very helpful with things like that. What was really there was an alternative theatre. That would have been very interesting in this town and we need it desperately.

You finally found the theatre you talked about that Canadians needed, a theatre in an old legion hall.

That was it. That worked very nicely. There was a lot of local opposition to it on the part of Americans and Britishers. They arrived, not always, but they arrived with the feeling that this is a colony so they should colonize it further. It did rather destroy my peace of mind when even Greg Curnoe would say, "Oh why didn't you put on *Ubu Roi* or LeRoi Jones' latest play about blacks taking over the University of Cleveland?" We didn't have any black actors and I didn't see the sense of putting it on. Period.

The MacIntyre Building is slated for demolition. You have been active in trying to prevent its destruction.

I don't know if they'll destroy the hotel or not. The Talbot Hotel was the headquarters for the Donnelly coach. They've already got one of the other Donnelly hotels, the Western Hotel.

They're still after the Donnellys. [Laughter.]

Peter Debarrats talked of this recently in the Free Press, that the town doesn't seem to know how to preserve its images and to preserve its identity. It's just helpless in the face of the real estate people.

Richard Stingle said that, when you were asked why the Donnellys were so successful, you replied that it was the poetry of the play.

Yes, oddly enough you got people saying, "We've never been to a play like this before." We got college reviewers saying, "We just shut our ears when the chorus was on. We can't stand poetry being spoken by more than one person at a time." Anyway, a lot of people said, "Gee that's the first time I ever heard choral stuff and it works." It's like a big cinemascope movie, only it's all done with sound, you see, and a lot of it is subliminal. They're not going to get everything the first time, but it's an experience, so that worked. You got poetic drama revived in a way that I think is different from what Eliot and Yeats were always talking about. They needed to have workshops with little kids of age six in Dublin and London. But I started off doing verse drama with

Killdeer and burnt my fingers because no one really cared, but then I found that you could with the choral stuff in its unified ...

What is fascinating about Performance Poems *is that you involve the audience, turning the poems into potential plays in which the audience is invited to discover their history and create poetry out of it.*

Well, thank you very much. The whole thing arose from the fact that quite often when I go to poetry readings some of the poems that people read don't come off too well when they're read aloud because they're meant to be read in your head. They're quiet, overheard kind of things and often quite difficult. You have to spend some time figuring them out. That's when you get these poets who will stand up to sort of explain the poem for you before they actually read it ... or half-teach it – that's the problem. Anyway, to my mind, you suddenly realize that there's a kind of poem that's an oral poem and is meant to be belted out and involve the audience. It's not quiet. It's not lyric. The most successful of these performance poems, "The Lament of the Poet," has generally gone over quite well when it's acted. And also the poem about swearing, the art of swearing, has gone over very well. Colleen and I did it. It's like a nightclub act, in effect. Some of the other poems haven't been done yet publicly, but they could involve high school kids or public school kids in choral situations with audiovisual.

There's a variety of interesting forms in this book: journal entries, drawings, emblems, musical scores and songs.

They reflect my own interests. Try everything you know, try all that can be tried. A lot of people that write poetry have no interest in music whatsoever, or drama. Get away from *personal expression*. Try *community expression*.

Performance Poems is a long tapestry of events which has a wide range: local, provincial, national, and international. I especially liked "The Party of the Year."

That was a poem commissioned for the CBC. I had my son and my daughter-in-law looking up rhymes for me and doing research on it because you were supposed to try and do cultural life in Canada in terms of a New Year's Party. It was great fun to get the hockey in there and the various other stupid funny things that happen. I think that was the year that the American soprano spectacularly failed to sing "O Canada" properly down in New York. But, the fascinating banality of Canadian life, as I think I told you, Laurence, was that Zena Cherry, on whom I did a take-off of her society columns in the *Globe*, wrote to me saying, "Oh I wish I had been to that party!" And do you know that more people read her in the *Globe* than anything else?

London, Ontario, July 23, 1991

Acknowledgements

I would like to thank France Smyth, who transcribed some of these interviews. I would also like to express my appreciation to Laura Estill, who proofread the manuscript. And I would especially like to thank my wife, Mary, who helped to edit this collection of interviews.

*

"An Interview with Ralph Gustafson." *Poetry Canada Review*. Summer, 1996.

"An Interview with George Johnston." *Zymergy*. Volume V, Number 2. Autumn, 1991.

"An Interview with P.K. Page." *The Museletter*. Winter, 1994/95.

"An Interview with Fred Cogswell." *ellipse*. Number 68. 2002.

"An Interview with Louis Dudek." *The River review / La Revue rivière*. Number 1, 1995.

Eternal Conversations: Remembering Louis Dudek. Montreal DC Books, 2003.

"An Interview with Al Purdy." *The Fiddlehead*. Number 204. Summer, 2000.

"Interview with Anne Szumigalski." *The Museletter*. Spring, 1994.

"Interview with James Reaney." *The River review / La Revue rivière*. Number 3, 1993.

Biographical Notes

Ralph Gustafson was born in Lime Ridge, Quebec, in 1909. He was educated at Bishop's University and later at Oxford University. He published thirty-seven volumes of poetry, and short stories, as well as three anthologies of Canadian poetry, winning the Governor General's Award for *Fire on Stone* in 1974. He died in 1995.

George Johnston was born in 1913 in Hamilton and graduated from the University of Toronto. From 1949 until his retirement in 1980, he taught Anglo-Saxon and Old Norse at Carleton University. He published numerous books of poems, and was well known for his translation of Old Norse and Faroese. He died in 2004.

P.K. Page had a remarkable career as a visual artist and poet. Born in Swanage in the south of England in 1916, she grew up in Calgary, worked in St. John and later moved to Montreal where she helped found *Preview*. She published more than ten volumes of poems and several books of fiction and non-fiction. She died in January, 2010, in Victoria, British Columbia.

Fred Cogswell was born in East Centreville, New Brunswick, in 1917. One of the most important of Canadian publishers, he published more than 300 titles for Fiddlehead Books. He wrote over thirty of his own volumes, edited anthologies and a number of literary articles and is also well known for his skillful translation of Quebec and Acadian writers. He died in Vancouver in 2004.

Louis Dudek, born in 1918 in Montreal, Quebec, and educated at McGill University and Columbia University, went on to teach at McGill for more than thirty years. He published more than thirty books of poetry and essays and edited some of the most influential magazines of the time, including Contact Press, CV2, Delta Canada, and DC books. Editor and critic Frank Davey wrote: "Louis Dudek has had the most influence on subsequent generations of Canadians." He died in Montreal in 2001.

Al Purdy helped to shape Canadian poetry for over thirty years. An autodidactic poet, he surged into prominence in the 1960s with his volume *Cariboo Horses*, which won the Governor General's Award. He published more than forty volumes of poetry, essays, a novel, and an autobiography. Not long before his death in 2000, he was awarded the Poet of the Land Award.

Anne Szumigalski was born in London, England in 1922, and immigrated to Canada after the Second World War. Instrumental in developing poetry in Saskatchewan, she also helped found the Saskatchewan Writers' Guild. She published more than fifteen books of poetry. She died in Saskatoon in 1999.

James Reaney, one of the most influential Canadian poets and playwrights, won the Governor General's Award for *The Red Heart*, *A Suit of Nettles*, and *Twelve Letters to a Small Town*. He published numerous plays and books of poems. From 1960-89, he taught at the University of Western Ontario. He died in June, 2008.

Printed on Rolland Enviro100, which contains 100% recycled post-consumer fibre, is EcoLogo, Processed Chlorine Free and FSC Recycled certified and manufactured using biogas energy.